THE SEVEN FACES
OF TIME

Books by Aleksandra Kasuba

Published by iUniverse

Private Heresies, 2000

Child Ticking, 2001

In the Wake of Dreams, 2001

THE SEVEN FACES OF TIME

Aleksandra Kasuba

iUniverse, Inc.
New York Lincoln Shanghai

THE SEVEN FACES OF TIME

Copyright © 2005 by Aleksandra Kasuba

iUniverse books may be ordered through booksellers or by contacting:

iUniverse
2021 Pine Lake Road, Suite 100
Lincoln, NE 68512
www.iuniverse.com
1-800-Authors (1-800-288-4677)

ISBN: 0-595-33536-5 (pbk)
ISBN: 0-595-66963-8 (cloth)

Printed in the United States of America

Contents

Introduction

I still remember the day I was told that the big clock in our house did more than make pleasant sounds—sixty ticks made up a minute, sixty minutes an hour, and twelve hours a day or a night. When I learned that people all over the world timed their daily activities by the same clock, time became my invisible companion. Our car would stop at an intersection, and I would wonder whether time ran ahead of us. If so, when would we catch up with it? Or why would the clock move so slowly when I had to wait for someone, but hours would slip by unnoticed when I was busy? My great-uncle's family set their clocks an hour earlier than standard time, which struck me as the boldest proclamation of independence from the world outside their house. Later I worried why the space-time continuum failed to make sense to me, as if the dash between space and time skipped over something essential.

By profession I am a visual artist. In 1970 I was building interactive environments and drawing up projects I hoped to build in the future. In one project, I explored the experiences of earth, water, fire, and air; and in 1975, when the project was published in a booklet *Utility for the Soul,* by Didymus Press in San Francisco, I wondered whether time could be investigated in a similar manner.

The idea is rooted in the fleeting confusion that occurs when one of two trains parked parallel in a station starts moving, and a passenger sitting inside one of them is not sure which train is in motion. To recreate the effect, I needed two movements to take place parallel to each other—one visual, the other moving the "passenger". By changing the direction and speed between them, I expected to evoke the sensations of being rushed forward or held back, moving in or out of synchrony with the world, or standing still while being in motion. I wished to create situations in which the experience of time would be palpable. Sketches of several installations convinced me that I would never see such complex machinery built and only described the projected experiences instead.

To my surprise, the imagined mechanical installations yielded seven distinct perceptions of time. I have outlined them in "The Physics of Metaphysics: Personal Musings," the article published in *The Journal of Mind and Behavior* (Winter 1998, Volume 19, Number 1, pages 65–90, with pages 85, 87, and 88 revised).

1. There is a time when the past and the future part ways and the present stops fleeting. It happens when I become other than myself—say, a pigeon strutting, straining to rise; or maybe a drop of water, swelling as the drop swells, rolling over as it does, and while hanging upside down, learning what every drop of water already knows. In this frame of mind, a myriad of appearances disguise the sameness in one and all. In the here and now, changes take place under the skin, like hot and cold, to mark the transition from one state to the other. By becoming "other," I take measure of myself. In the absolute now, the world is a mirror held up to me, and I am a mirror to all.

2. Time flows like a river when the world shatters into separate things: all are carried by time, from the past into the future, in a steady progression of changes. In this time frame, time and change conspire, rendering everything separately mutable. If I stand still, oppressive changes pile up around me. If

I resist the onslaught, the fight is upstream all the way, the effort futile. And if I drift along, the undertows pull me under. In linear time, only memories and dreams are reliable.

3. And there comes a time when time seems less imposing, the changes seem less intrusive. From the safety of my niche I take action and using time as a free commodity, like water or air, I start rearranging things. I introduce changes that might improve my lot, and the availability of time gives me a grip on change itself. In this mind-set, days are a string of right and wrong actions: every intentional deed is a black or red entry in the balance sheet of gains and losses. The future itself is but an event in the making; the present is only a means of getting there.

4. Every so often, the futility of human arrangements shocks me into a standstill. In this state, nothing makes sense anymore: What is the rush? Where to? What is the fuss and bustle all about? In the end, what difference does it make how I amuse myself in the meantime? Yet to sit back and do nothing while memories of an active self disturb the present, and the present undermines the future is not easy either. And as the world moves on as usual, trapped in an immensity of time, I stagnate. The slightest prospect of change now strikes me like the promise of a spectacular escape—an unexpected deliverance from annihilation.

5. I am in personal time when I sense a clock ticking inside me. It strikes the hour when change recommends itself. And with a sense of self in motion, I gravitate from change to

change as confluences of inner and outer events deliver endings into beginnings. When nothing tugs or pulls, I wait and listen. And after completing a set number of revolutions, the inner clock strikes again—directing my attention, urging me to move on. On this path of least resistance, change is the vehicle. While time marks durations of distances, change in time delivers me to where I belong.

6. I am in circular time when days string together like beads on the loop of time. On some days I slip back to where I was many times before, going through the same motions, sifting through the same thoughts. On other days I slide forward, getting ahead of myself, yet I am not going any place in particular. Routine is where the self and the world intersect. Change is the keeper of the patterns I am learning to read. In circles, small and immense, everything is becoming something else—either more or less of itself, or part of some other thing. In circular time nothing is ever gained or lost or wasted, not even my own insignificant life.

7. Once in a while, timelessness alights with energy spilling forth like a fountain turned on full force. Seized by the gush—surrendering to the moment at hand—in this fissure of time, I am an instrument of the energy that is rushing through me but not acting upon me. Yet whatever I touch is changed: in the absence of time, I am an agent of change. And through the changes I make, I receive gifts unasked for, brought forth by the sap that splits the seed, the bud, the bloom, or keeps the planets in orbit.

Almost thirty years have passed since I first described the seven perceptions of time. And ever since then I have kept an eye on whether other people have made similar observations. Though comparable inner states abound in literature, especially in poetry, none are linked to the experience of time. The above seven perceptions of time appear to be unprecedented; thus no footnotes, endnotes, or source notes are available. *The Seven Faces of Time* is a personal account of an artist's inquiry; namely, how by adjusting to external events, an individual not only changes his or her perception of time, but also realigns the outlook, the mindset, and the mode of behavior.

To incite thought, rather than challenge a reader's prevailing convictions, I have incorporated the above observations in an allegorical journey. The dreamlike episodes take a restless adolescent girl through the seven experiences of time outlined above. In each episode, she is in the same surroundings but relates to them differently: an altered perception of time makes her see home and herself through a different lens. Questioning every shift in outlook against her own experience, the girl goes on, assured that she is merely sampling the options life has to offer. In her adult life, she finds that switches in her perspective occur daily, the practice saving her much frustration. Finally, her youthful ramblings have begun to make sense.

To highlight a point in an episode, some dream events are quoted from *In the Wake of Dreams*, the narrative in verse published by iUniverse in 2001.

It is my hope that in reading *The Seven Faces of Time,* the reader will notice that the fleeting and effortless shifts in thought and behavior we practice daily, as if by habit, are triggered by interactions that evoke the experience of time; that the changes in outlook are neither accidental nor fixed but adjustable by choice.

A. K.
New Mexico, November 2004.

1

On Home Grounds

Having nothing better to do on a Friday night, I said goodnight to Mom and Dad and walked to Mary's house. When I arrived, Betty was braiding Carry's hair, Martha was painting her toenails purple, and Linda was spreading a black T-shirt on the bed. I walked over to look at it and counted eleven small white skulls aligned across the front of the T-shirt.

"Delicious…" crooned Linda. "Mary, where did you get this creepy thing?"

I didn't hear her answer, for when I looked up, the room was drained of color and frozen in time. An uncanny feeling compelled me to say, "I have to go…"

The girls looked at me, their stunned faces also frozen in black and white.

"Alya, you just got here!" Mary's voice came from afar.

"I better…" I whispered, and backed out of the room, as if unsure of what to expect. The doorknob felt cold and real, and as I slipped out, I heard "gee-whizzes" laced with Linda's nervous giggle exploding in that otherworldly air.

Running home in the warm September night, I wondered what was happening to me. Stopping in a pool of light, I recalled last Friday at Linda's house when the world had also turned snapshot still, but when I had blinked, all returned to normal. Not this time. This time the fixation had taken hold, and I knew that nothing would ever be the same.

I was about to cross the street, but when I envisioned myself coming home sooner than expected—Mom's questioning eyes, Dad looking up from his paper—not yet, I thought and sat down under the maple tree.

The rustle of leaves was soothing; the coarse trunk against my back drained away the dread. Sifting through the events of the evening, I realized that for some time now I had felt reluctant to go to these girlish gatherings; I enjoyed the hours spent by myself more than those with people. To tell the truth, I felt no need to talk, no need to even listen to the intimate chattering the girls so gleefully enjoyed. Something wasn't right. When I was alone, a sweet longing welled up inside me—as if a bubble were about to burst and propel me into a world brimming with excitement. Savoring the feeling, I walked home and went straight to bed.

That night I dreamt of an old map, a faded round mass of land surrounded by turbulent waters. An eerie glow at the center of the map made it hard to see what was there, but near the top was a small garden encircled by a fence. Inside it a naked man and a woman were holding an apple between them. Four rivers flowed from the garden, with walled cities crowding their banks, and the mountains between them raging with beasts. At the bottom of the map the four rivers converged, spilling into the waters that encircled the round landmass. In the churning waters a towering, black mountain jutted straight up and on top of the mountain, in a nest of flames, a huge petrified egg.

I was looking at the egg when the mountain rumbled, and it shook the egg so hard that it cracked open. A large, featherless hatchling stood up wobbling, and as it shivered, waves of white feathers sprouted. When it spread its wings, it rose high into the air like a promise and vanished in the map's glowing center.

A sleepy silence blanketed the faceless horizon. Only a step away from where I stood, clouds were spinning slowly, sucking me in.

"Don't move. I know the way out of here," said a white sparrow hovering above me.

"What is this? Where am I?"

"At the outer edge of your present state," twittered the bird.

"And you?"

"I am your other, the one you talk to when you talk to yourself."

"What is happening?" I asked.

"The world you live in has lost its power to move you. Follow me and you'll see the same familiar things, as if for the first time."

"Must I?" I asked, not sure whether I wanted to go through another ordeal.

"Those who dream the map are destined to take this journey. But not everyone reaches the end of the road, the place where shadows lift."

Curious about the shadows, I said, "Yes, I want to know what lies ahead."

"What you are about to see is not your future. *Change in time* is what the journey is about." Alighting on my shoulder, the white sparrow chirped, "Turn around!"

Before us lay desolate flatlands. The sky was the color of ashes as bleak as the ground under my feet. There were no trees, no mountains, no landmarks of any sort to suggest a direction.

"What you see is a reflection of your mind," whispered the sparrow.

A chill ran up my spine and I stopped.

The bird twittered, "Go on, there is nothing else we can do."

With my eyes fixed on the horizon, I walked on, but finding myself walking in circles and feeling lost in this no-man's-land, I stopped again.

"Look at your feet," whispered the bird into my ear.

There was nothing there to look at but a small dust devil whirling near by.

"Look again, what looks like nothing may take us out of here," the bird continued.

Now the dust devil was twisting around my ankles, and, as I looked at it, a forked tongue stuck out to sample the air. "It's a lizard," I thought, and a reptilian belly, born in thought, rubbed against my shin. Whirling slower, the dust devil grew bigger. "The thing must be alive," crossed my mind, and that instant a snout appeared sniffing my scent. "I better stop guessing," I thought, for every time I tried to guess what was inside the dust, an image of it appeared. It was as if my thoughts were shaping the thing. But instead of going away, the whirling mass heaved like a four-legged animal rising to its feet: a green-scaled tail fell to one side, a claw groped for ground—

"It's a dragon!" I shouted, scaring away the bird.

Sure enough, a full-fledged dragon with slime-green scales stood up gasping for air. This, then, was how the world looked to me.

I jumped aside but the dragon saw me. Exhaling curlicues of flames, eyes flashing white, the creature took a step closer. With nowhere to run or hide, I pulled off the braided bracelet Mary had given me and tossed it at the dragon. Catching it in midair, it swallowed the morsel in one gulp, and it grew bigger twofold. Hungry for more, nostrils spewing steam, the dragon took another step. Slipping off the ring Mom had given me for my birthday, I threw it at the beast, but that too failed to appease it. The golden locket willed to me by Grandmother was my most precious possession, and when it, too, vanished in the beast's jaws, the dragon grew monstrously big. Roaring triumphantly, it exhaled another batch of flames and—mouth gaping, tail thrashing—reached for my head. When its tail swished between us, I grabbed it and shoved it into its gaping jaws, and the dragon swallowed it. Its eyes bulged with surprise, its body twisted in a ring, and it froze. I jumped onto the dragon's belly, slipped through the ring, slid down the other side, and ran without looking back.

Catching up with me, the sparrow shrieked into my ear, "Stop! This will not do! You must start at the beginning!"

I stopped and turned around—where the dragon had stood, a tall rainbow now lit up the gloomy sky.

"There it is!" chirped the bird excitedly. "Go for it! It may vanish any moment!"

Running as fast as I could, I ran into the rainbow. The colors splashed in my face, and I stopped. Seeing me puzzled, the bird explained.

"You must enter the unknown not by accident, but fully aware that you are taking a decisive step. Only then will you know why you are where you are. Don't fret, you won't be alone." Then it whispered, "Try the color purple on your left, or is it on your right? Never mind, just go. It does not matter where you start."

2

In the Here and Now

On the other side of purple, Dad was mowing the lawn by the lilac bushes; the swing on the porch was swaying in the breeze, and the curtains in my bedroom window were billowing in and out. Everything was in its proper place, yet different. The silence was ocean deep, the whole scene swaying as things do underwater. When the curtains in the bay window moved aside, the face in the window looked familiar, but when I approached it, I was startled. It was my own face—eyes wide open—skinny me, wearing the off-white sleeveless dress with the small buttons at the neckline unbuttoned.

Spooked by the image, I quickly averted my eyes, and my gaze landed on the potted geraniums on the front steps. A sensation of falling into red—into rivers of red meandering lazily through the mysteries of color—made me blink. And next I was gazing into a morning glory cup, sampling the delight of blues as insects do. Riding blue thermals, I was soaring deliriously when a passing fly buzzed a piercing alarm. At once iron-heavy, I started falling. I was sinking through ever denser and darker layers of blue, landing on a twig gently swaying in a purple shadow. In the elbow of a leaf, a drop of dew quivered, and as the drop swelled, I swelled; and as the drop rolled under, I rolled with it. Hanging upside down, I learned what every drop of water knows already: the pull of gravity is stronger than any grip. Seeing the drop stretch to a break-off point, I shut my eyes.

And so it was throughout, whatever I looked at, I became. Thus when a cat stalking a pigeon caught my eye, I could not help but be the cat. As the cat froze, I became the pigeon—learning how it feels to fly. A neighbor called, "Here kitty, kitty! Here kitty!" and the voice struck me like a drum—the swirl of sensations making me gasp for air.

Smothered by the onslaught of impressions, I leaned against a tree and my skin turned to bark, my arms flailing like branches and fingers exploding in clusters of leaves. When under the weight of green I slumped onto a stone, I turned to stone, and when the scent of lilacs invaded my petrified body, the aroma touched the deepest recesses of my being. With a shudder I realized that though trapped in my personal human disguise, I was no different from the rest of creation. In the here and now I was taking measure of myself—I, a mirror to the world, and the world, a mirror held up to me.

The sound of a voice made me start.

"Didn't I say that familiar things may look the same but hold much more than meets the eye?"

Alighting on my shoulder and hopping from foot to foot with excitement, the white sparrow asked, "Did anything strike you as peculiar when you were changing identities, turning into something other than yourself?"

I had difficulty remembering. "Peculiar? Not really. It felt as if the curtains of time had parted to let me in, then closed behind me. There was a *before*, like before falling asleep, and an *after*, like after awakening in the morning. What happened in between happened as if in a dream." Looking straight at the bird, I asked, "Am I still dreaming?"

"Yes, in a way, you are. But this is a waking dream."

As if in confirmation, the entire front yard burst into a spectacle of colors. Unable to take it in, yet eager to remember, I picked up the whole scene by the corners like a sheet of cloth, and tying the corners together, I clutched the bundle to my chest. With my eyes firmly shut, I placed one foot in front of the other and started walking, the bundle of sensations humming softly, leading me on. I dared open my eyes again only when the vibrant bundle fell silent.

I stood at the edge of a birch forest.

"Shall we enter?" I asked the white sparrow on my shoulder.

"Remember the dragon you saw in your mind and it came to be? You outsmarted the beast without a sword in hand. When you switched identities with things, you escaped the onslaught of sensations by shutting your eyes. What happens to you next also depends on what you make of what you see."

Feeling good about myself, I looked at the forest again. The canopy of whispering leaves offered shelter; the pungent green scent was invigorating, and the luster bouncing off the thicket of pearly trunks made shadows transparent.

"Let's go," I said.

The bird shook its head. "I prefer to stay out of forests," it said. "But you go on, for this part of the journey you'll want to be alone."

Leaving my shoulder, the bird circled my head once and flew off. I picked my way through the first line of trees, and the farther I walked into the forest, the safer I felt. When I came to a clearing and saw—suspended in a shadow—green specks swaying, I decided that this was the place to take stock of what was happening to me. With a stone in hand, I split the sturdy shadows into planks, and with them I built a hut, a table, a bench, and a bed. In the sunniest spot of the clearing, I dug up a patch of earth and planted rows of wild onions, leafy greens, and barley for the winter months.

I was not alone. Every morning the sun rolled over the treetops shaking loose rainbows of dew. While the sun stayed, we chatted and exchanged news.

"Good morning," the sun would say, breathless after climbing the trees.

"Good morning," I would reply. "How is the weather outside the forest?"

"It is cloudy in Nevada, still raining in New Jersey, and sunny in your hometown."

"Any news back home?"

"Nothing in particular. Your mother has the sniffles, and your father is wearing new shoes."

"Do they miss me?"

"Nobody misses you because everyone lives in a dream world of their own. Your adventures do not interfere with theirs." And after a sneeze, "That is, as long as you, Alya, are feeling all right, not home-sick or desperate. If you are, I urge you to go home."

"I'm fine," I would say, wondering why the sun kept talking about me going home.

Then together we would tend the garden; I would weed the patch, and the sun would paint green every budding leaf.

"Are you sure you're fine?" the sun might inquire before leaving.

"I wouldn't exchange this for anything in the world. The peace and quiet here are truly enjoyable, and solitude brings me great comfort."

The other day the sun asked me, "Don't you ever feel lonely?"

"Why should I? You visit me every day, birds stop to look in, things grow, and rotating shadows keep time. There is much to do and much to think about and no time for feeling sad or lonely. I am happy here."

The sun smiled, "I know…See you tomorrow!" And climbing up steps of shadows, the sun would continue on her way.

Left alone, I would inhale the hour and sing to a cloud passing overhead or a leaf swaying in the breeze. In that intimate space of being, everything I sang to listened, and I heard each in turn. In song I gave something away and, in return, received something; the exchange stitched the world and me together.

All was cozy and well until the morning when I noticed that someone was eating the shoots in my garden. The place was safe no more. To keep the nibblers away, I felled a great number of trees and built a sturdy birch trunk stockade to protect my domain.

Several nights later, I was awakened by the thundering noise of wild creatures running around the stockade—thumping noises signaling attempted break-ins. To prevent a surprise stampede, the next morning I started spinning grass and cobwebs together, making cords that stretched from points in the stockade to the four corners of my pillow. The softly humming memory bundle comforted my head at night. Next, I hung on the lines dry seedpods as rattles, to give me ample warning in case the wild creatures broke in.

After weeks of spinning cord, it was almost impossible to move about inside my enclave. I had entrapped myself in such a dense tangle of warnings, so sensitive to touch, that every so often I'd set off an alarm, scaring myself silly. And still, night after night, the wild creatures thundered and circled the place.

One night, I was up late watching moonlight and shadow change places. My thoughts were folding and unfolding, ascending a moonbeam, then plunging to the abysmal depths of a shadow; then grooving ahead or burrowing deeper; thoughts crossing each other in darkness, meandering in circles, turning on themselves again and again. Like the unbroken path of a bird in flight, my mind was a tangle. For since the sun had asked me whether I was lonely, I'd been thinking about it.

Lost in thought, I did not notice the moon leaning out of the sky and watching me. When I looked up, he was spreading his star-studded kingly robes on the treetops and reclining, with his head propped on an elbow.

"Amazing, isn't it, how night thoughts differ from day thoughts?" he said, his deep voice rolling softly in the darkness. "Even thoughts have another side to them. Would you agree?"

My line of thought broken, I asked, "Why must everything be so complicated? Why can't my thoughts stay on track, instead of twisting and running in circles? Nothing is predictable anymore. I have no idea what to expect tomorrow—what's going to happen next—It really frightens me to think that nothing can be relied on or trusted." I paused, then proceeded cautiously, "When you make your rounds at night, do you see the creatures that make those horrible noises outside the stockade and keep me awake night after night?"

"Noises? I hear no noises when I look in on you at night; I see no creatures running around the stockade or threatening you in any way." Seeing that I was not convinced, the moon asked, "Is that what you think?"

"I hear them, and I know that I am in danger! Am I not to believe my own ears?" Then, somewhat hesitantly I asked, "Are thoughts unreliable too?"

"Of course they are unreliable. In the here and now, thoughts follow what goes on around you. You see water, you think of water. You catch a whiff of a smell and wonder what is there. You hear a fly, and you think of flying or buzzing or the insect's nasty bite. Your thoughts try to make sense of what you see and hear and touch and smell. But since thoughts are impressions translated into words, in the translation, many unexpected things happen. Verbal interpretation is the trickiest part of your mind." Ready to leave, the moon stood up.

"Do you mean thoughts can be just as overwhelming and misleading as sensations?"

"Yes, that's what I'm saying. Danger has many disguises! Stay well!" With a nod, the moon gathered up the spray of moonbeams and rolled out of sight.

Alone in the dark, I called out to the invisible creatures. "Stop ruining my life! There are plenty of wild onions and greens out there for you to feast on. Why do you have to eat mine?" The night soaked up the sound of my voice and I felt better.

The following night, the thunder of hooves was dimmer than the night before. I got up, stepped outside, and called out again.

"I mean no harm, I have taken nothing from you, and I ask nothing of you in return." My words dissolved in the velvety darkness.

"Why can't you leave me alone?" Not a leaf stirred.

"Let's live in peace!" I shouted. Still silence reigned supreme.

Satisfied, I went back to bed. But now the word *peace* was ringing bells in my head, keeping me awake late into the night.

The next morning I woke up to a world where every leaf and streak of light, even my bundle of memories, was staring back at me. Was I the culprit? Had I imagined the ferocious beasts—heard noises in my head? Had I built defenses against nonexistent offenders and raised the whole ruckus myself? Imagine—I'd built a stockade to last a hundred years; the network of alarms was intricate enough to spot a passing fly!

Had fear gotten the better of me?

Then and there, I knew that defenses do not make you stronger. By shutting out the world, I had just invented another. Runaway thoughts had taken over my life, just as sensory impressions had done it before.

Curious as to what lay outside the stockade, I climbed it and could hardly believe what I saw: there was no forest, only stumps of the trees I'd felled to build the stockade. Among the up-shoots of grass, a white steed grazed; the sun-drenched scene was so serene that I jumped to the steed's side.

The magnificent white steed stood there trembling—hide bristling—as if it was ordained to stand still. Thunderous forebodings shattered the air as I approached it teasing, "Come now, come..." The sky was rip-roaring no! no! when I reached to stroke its silken belly murmuring, "Hush, hush now." And when I touched the steed, it stood stock-still. Leaning forward, I whispered into its velvety ear, "Teach me how not to think."

3

In the River of Time

Home no longer felt like home, but like a place empty of life. Moving in a world I no longer cared about, I began to see myself as a robot—programmed to function the same way for years to come.

Seeking excitement outside the house, I started hanging out with a new set of friends after school. It was a rougher crowd. Every other word was a curse. When putting down the adults in our lives, we made fun of what they thought and how they lived. These kids were ready to experiment with everything, including drugs and sex. My parents said little, yet their anxious glances disturbed me. I never doubted that they loved me or that I loved my mom and dad. That was established, but it was no longer enough to keep me tied to home. There was a world out there to be explored, experiences to be had and shared, so much to investigate and learn. In order to think for myself, I had to distance myself from my parents.

One evening after a downpour, I was walking home from a friend's house with my gaze fixed on the water running in the gutter, when suddenly I saw myself in a river as wide as life itself. The here and now was no longer a chain of perpetual blinks, but one continuous flow that moved everything on earth in the same direction—from the past into the future.

A bewitching dusk hung over the river. In it, I was pushed and pummeled and kicked by all in whose way I happened to drift. The stronger people were pushing the weaker ones out of their way, climbing over their heads, some clinging to others, some struggling to break loose. Every person was fighting tooth and nail to stay afloat, but the river was indifferent, swift, and unruffled by what went on inside it.

Wanting no part of it—appalled by what I saw—I gave in to the current and was carried to the fringes of the river, where the helpless and the hopeless floated like flotsam. In these crowded backwaters, hushed wailings and faint screams stifled the air. When the long arm of an undertow reached for me and started pulling me under, I thought it was the end; the thought enveloped me like a warm blanket. But when someone kicked me in the face, I grabbed the foot and was towed into a swiftly moving midstream current.

I did not fare much better there either, for I was yelled at and battered by those whose progress I obstructed. In this river, the laws of the mob prevailed, and though all the people were facing the same predicament, each struggled separately. Seeing how cruel people are to each other when survival is at stake, I was faint with exhaustion and about to give in and go under when someone took hold of my hand.

Facing me was a woman with a deep olive complexion and graying hair. "You must be new here," she said.

"I am...I've never seen people this mean, this rude. How can anybody survive such horrors? Is there a way out of here?"

"There is. Some people make it and some don't. Most don't even look for other ways of living; people stay in this river because they don't know any better."

In spite of what was going on around us, the woman looked calm and composed.

"Have you been in here long?" I asked.

"I actually came back to look for my daughter. We haven't heard from her in several years..." After a pause she added, "You reminded me of her...the way she was when she left home."

"Why would anyone want to stay here?" I asked.

"Sooner or later everyone falls into the River of Time and gets stuck in it. Here things are at the mercy of change, its nimble fingers alter each thing separately, and change pushes all to oblivion."

I looked at the people around me, shoving and hitting each other. "But how do they survive this?"

"By staying out of harm's way. Those who learn the rules of the game learn how to secure a position in these treacherous waters."

"Secure a position? Here?"

"Have you noticed that you are less battered than when you first fell into the river?"

I nodded.

"It's because I am looking for my daughter, and I have a clear-cut objective to guide me. I'm neither beating those who bump into us, nor pushing aside the ones who come too close. In these waters, it is wise to keep to yourself; and if you leave people alone, they'll leave you alone. We're proceeding smoothly because I am aiming for the empty spaces and swimming in the gaps unoccupied by others. You must have noticed that everyone here cares only for himself and the rest be damned. That's what life comes down to when people are looking for some kind of stronghold to ease their struggle."

"Stronghold?"

"Look and you'll see what I mean."

Raising my head, I looked around, but what I saw was a river filled with people in water up to their chins, heads bobbing up and down on the surface. Some were by themselves, some held together as if by threads, and some were clustered in awkward positions, with their arms and legs entwined. Farther down, a mass of people bearing a man on their shoulders was ruthlessly plowing through the thick of humanity.

A corpse floated by face down. No one paid attention.

The woman pulled me closer. "See that small cluster of people with children riding on their shoulders? It's a family; the kids are observing how the parents maneuver, and all are moving along nicely. The parents' stronghold is in the future of their children, for if their children do well, the parents will have it that much easier."

"See the group behind them turning round and round? They are infighting, as if arguments could prevent them from going under. Every member knows what needs to be done to keep the group afloat, yet everyone wants the other to take the responsibility; they blame each other for the misery they suffer. Since no one is watching the stream that carries them, they drift—unaware of where they are or where they are headed."

"And those two over there—see the one holding the other's arm and that one struggling to pull herself free? Sooner or later, the pull and tear will wear them both down."

"And who are they?" I asked, pointing to the massive cluster of people pushing everyone out of their way.

"Hangers-on. See the man riding on their shoulders? Those who have raised him to this position have no vision of their own and follow the personal vision of the appointed leader. Having entrusted their lives to him, they will cater to all his whims as long as he pleases the many. Look!"

And as she spoke, we saw the man pulled down from on high. "See the mass crumbling, infighting, and dispersing? That's what happens to hangers-on. Not used to thinking for themselves, they flounder aimlessly until they find someone to lead them. You pay dearly for letting others take responsibility for your life and suffer endless indignation for it. There are no free rides here. As a matter-of-fact, no free rides anywhere."

"Is competition the key to survival?"

"Not really. Anyway, not in the River of Time where nothing stands still, and change affects everybody in one way or another. Those who compete may gain a short-lived advantage here and there, but never enough to lead them out of here. To survive in this river, you need to have a goal to aim for and to guide you; or you are doomed to flounder in this soup of humanity, merely responding to what goes on right under your nose."

After a pause she added, "You are too young to know what you want out of life. You haven't seen enough of the world to form a vision of your own to chart your future by. Be patient, it will come."

I caught sight of a man, on some kind of floating devise, paddling against the current and shouting. "And who is he?"

"That fellow has lost all sense of direction. Paddling upstream, he actually stays in the same place all the time. What keeps him going are the slogans he shouts, 'People stand up!' 'Fight for your rights!' 'You are the future!' His contraption is guaranteed to sink the minute he stops shouting." Then she added, "And yet, in times when the hangers-on take up most of the space, people like him cut open channels through which many slip by unnoticed."

Another corpse floated by. Pockets full of air and silence.

"You said there is a way out of here." I ventured to remind the good woman.

"See these fast swimmers moving through the thick of it, as if nothing stands in their way? Knowing how to swim helps, but even the best swimmers may not make it out of here. Watch the one on the left. I can tell already that he's not going to make it far, because with furtive glances he keeps measuring his progress against those who swim beside him. Were he to lift his head, he'd see that others are overtaking them. It's what you compare yourself to that determines your own progress. Life is not a race, it is a chance given to all; and unless you know the basics of the game, your chances are slim."

"Can you tell who might go the distance?"

"See the one swimming off center at a pace most suitable to her? She is not distracted by what happens on her right or left, or ahead or behind her, but swims steadily ahead, unwavering in her path. This happens only to those who have a steadfast aim fixed in their minds. Their vision is their stronghold."

"Is their struggle over when they reach the target?"

"You mean, once they are outside the usual grind and hustle of survival? Though the common stresses and discomforts the rest of us suffer are no longer on their minds, they still have to protect what they have—whether it is the position they hold or the vision itself. They are not free of hassles, for the peace of mind they enjoy, which imposes a new set of restrictions on them, needs to be tended to and guarded from day-to-day."

"Is there anything left for them to wish for?"

"Everyone wishes for happiness, and when the setup seems just right, many find that pursuits of happiness are just as finicky and

short-lived as anything else in life. Having spent their lives in securing the basic necessities, they are apt to discover a gnawing spiritual
unrest that upsets the good life, and once the suspicion creeps in
that they might have missed or overlooked something in life…"

She froze, eyes riveted on a group to the left of us.

"The redhead! She looks like…my daughter!" Before letting go of
my hand, she said, "Good luck!" And diving ahead, she vanished in
the mass of bobbing heads.

Taking a cue from her, paying no attention to others I aimed
straight for the opposite bank of the river and reached solid ground
in no time. As I climbed out of the water, I felt something bumping
about my ankles—the bundle of memories had washed up beside
me.

After climbing the steep, slippery bank, I looked around. Before
me lay a lush, green, wide-open meadow; gentle breezes combing
the tall grass; a procession of clouds drifting in a predestined direction; and the song of a lark stitching heaven and earth together.
Moved by the simplicity of things untouched by human hands, I
entered the meadow ready to embrace the world anew.

I had taken only a few steps when my foot slipped. The ground
under the cover of grass was uneven. Several steps farther I stumbled
again then fell into a dark and narrow shaft, too deep for me to
climb out. Keeping watch over the opening high above me, I listened for signs of life, but only grass rustled in the wind.

"Help!" I shouted timidly, echoes of my voice fading into silence.

Sitting at the bottom of the shaft, my gaze was fixed on the green-
streaked patch of blue above me. I listened to water rushing underground—ominous sounds pulsing in the dirt walls around me. Lost

to the world, I held the bundle of memories close to me; my past was all I had to hold on to.

Hearing footsteps, I called out again, and I stood up in time to see a young man spread the blades of grass and look over the edge.

"You called for help?" he asked.

"I did! Can you get me out of here?" I shouted.

"Let me see…You picked yourself a deep hole to fall into. Don't worry, you're not alone, the meadow is full of holes, and many people are trapped in them. In a situation like this, you should not be alone," said the stranger, positioning himself to jump in.

"Oh no! Don't jump!" I begged him, "Get help! Do something! Please!" Seeing his determination, I slumped to the ground.

"I'll keep you company," he said and jumped in, sitting down across from me—our knees touching.

He introduced himself. "I'm Jimmy. Welcome to our territory!"

"I'm Alya. I didn't know the meadow was full of treacherous holes. I could have broken my leg."

"Complaining already?" he asked, eyes keenly prying, as if he were a student of important matters. "The meadow looked so luscious, so inviting—you could not resist the temptation, right?"

Rumbling sounds forced us to lock our eyes.

"What was that?"

"It's the River of Time. Here it runs underground, no one knows how deep below the surface. When it rumbles like that, it's best to ignore it. Once in a while, you'll hear water rushing, but it's usually silent. And that's even worse, because this invisible river is more treacherous than the one above the ground. Here you don't see the dangers coming at you; they simply creep up on you unnoticed." Jimmy's voice hushed, as if he were telling me a secret.

"Is there a way out of this hole?" I asked also whispering.

Brushing dirt off his pants, he changed the subject. "So you crossed the big river all right. Isn't it something what people are willing to put up with? Nothing on earth is more stupid, more ignorant, and more selfishly hell-bound than humankind. Altogether, I find this business of living very disagreeable."

"How did you get here?"

"Alone in the big river, I was about to go under when I bumped into what felt like a sturdy root, and figuring I was near the shore, I grabbed it and climbed out—" A thunderous rumble made him stop. With his eyes steady on my face, Jimmy continued, "—only to wallow in mud for a long time. When I finally made it to firm ground and escaped the dredges of humanity, I too saw the meadow, and the spread looked promising. But like you, I also fell into a pit. At first I was disappointed, as you must be now, but nowadays, I'd rather talk to someone like you than take part in those morbid struggles above the ground!"

Sounds of water falling and churning filled the pit. They prompted me to say something, and raising my voice, I said, "Then you see no purpose in this?"

"Purpose! Does misery have a purpose? Misery is the same everywhere—why look for it? Why suffer endless humiliation or put up with struggles that only sap your energy and drag you down? No thanks. I'm a fast learner," he said loudly, brushing the dirt off his sleeve.

"Aren't you curious about what life has to offer?" I shouted to be heard.

"You've got to be kidding!" Jimmy shouted back. "Life has nothing more to offer than more of the same struggle, and what's the purpose in that?"

The wall of dirt by Jimmy's shoulder started crumbling, and soon a hand appeared, groping the air.

"Is that you, Auntie?" Jimmy sounded relieved.

"You here already?" asked a high-pitched, cracking voice, and the head of a woman emerged, dirt caking her face. "What's up? What's the underground rumbling about?"

"Auntie, meet Alya!" And turning to me, Jimmy said, "Down here, we get around; the place is riddled with tunnels connecting pit to pit. Life underground is not as dull as you might think!"

By then Auntie had dug through, and in the dim light of the pit, I was taken aback by her leathery face, which was fixed in an unpleasant grin.

"Hi! Welcome to our world!" she said, her eyes examining me intently as she wiggled between us.

"I do not intend to stay—" I began, but Auntie's hardened face, leaning into mine, stopped me short.

"Let me tell you, none of us did at first." While the underground river grumbled insistently, Auntie raised her fists and shouted, "Oh, shut up, let me talk to this creature—haven't seen one so young for years!"

To my surprise, the river did shut up, but now an iron-hard stillness encased us. Auntie looked up and down, sized up the pit, sized up me, and broke the silence. "You picked yourself a beauty to fall into, wouldn't you say so, Jimmy?"

"Beginner's luck!" Jimmy answered, and they both burst out laughing. I was not amused.

"Do people dig these pits themselves?" I hardly dared to ask.

"Of course they do," whispered Jimmy, as if afraid to be over-heard, "and some of the pits are ancient, dug deeper and deeper by generations of people. The truly desperate are the best at it—and also the most obsessed—for they are convinced that if they dig deep enough, they will reach the river, and then all will be well again. But it never works, for as you dig deeper, you reach a point when the dirt you throw out starts falling back onto your head, and that's the end of digging. That is, unless you want to bury yourself alive!" The two burst out laughing again.

"It happens, it certainly happens," said Auntie, and turning to Jimmy, she said, "The place is riddled with the best intentions, right?"

Jimmy nodded and his voice took on an edge. "Right. And there are plenty of good intentions to go around. Down here, the mind is truly inventive—imagination crackles, cranking out the most elaborate ways to escape the drudgeries of life. Our way of living is by far the best—above the ground they put you on a merry-go-round until the machinery breaks down!" he said, vigorously brushing his other sleeve.

Auntie sighed, "A conveyer belt, that's what it is up there. The merciless progression of changes is what grinds you to a pulp. Up there, if you manage to stand still, changes pile up around you so high that you are buried alive. If you resist the onslaught of changes, the fight is upstream all the way; and instead of getting anywhere, you simply reach exhaustion. Drift along, and you risk being pulled under. And yet the world goes on, as if there were nothing to it. Right?"

"Right," agreed our studious companion leaning back. "You see, down here we avoid the crunch by distancing ourselves from it all. Who says one has to take part in this grim bottomless struggle? Down here we don't put up with the injustices, indignations, and indifferences of life, because we have found a way to beat the system. 'Let them be,' I say. Retreat and you're in a different ballpark altogether. Let those who enjoy clawing at each other's gut do their dirty work. Here at last we're free to live as we please."

Auntie looked at me sternly. "When you think about it, you'll see that only dimwits take this monstrous river seriously."

"But how do you survive in this underground darkness, this isolation?" I asked, already thinking that their kind of life was no better than the one in the river above the ground.

"We feed off each other," said Auntie, and, leaning into my face again, she asked, "Admit it, our presence is comforting, no?"

I drew back, "It's not comfort I am looking for…I want to get out of here. I must go on."

"She must go on!" The two were in stitches again.

Looking away to escape their mockery, I glanced up, and there was a face staring down at us.

"Need help?" the stranger asked.

"Yes! Please! Get us out of here!" I shouted, standing up.

"I'll be right back!" said the stranger and disappeared.

Jimmy and Auntie exchanged glances and, clapping their hands and slapping their knees, enjoyed another spell of laughter.

"See what we mean?" said Auntie, catching her breath. "He won't be back. That's how people are. They promise anything to get you off their back, and that's the last you hear from them. At least down here we make ourselves useful by welcoming newcomers like you. Believe me, what people call living up there isn't worth the effort."

With his voice drifting, Jimmy said, "I would say that only the grandest dreams are worth the trouble." He spoke looking downcast, his fingers fixing the nonexistent pleats in his jeans. "But since that's not in the offing, the best life has to offer is to have someone like you two to talk to—people who have stared misery in the face and know how humiliating life can be."

Auntie chimed in, "And who know how to avoid the entanglements life sucks you into!"

"But I haven't seen *that* much misery to feel *that* hopeless," I said in a low voice.

"You must understand," Auntie responded quickly, "it's not hope we are talking about here. It's about having a mind sharp enough to cut through the muck dished out on every street corner—intended to tame and harness you for good, to make a dummy out of you. Don't you understand? It's about seeing what life is really all about." And again she leaned her face into mine. Seeing me cringe, Jimmy intervened.

"Pay attention to what she says—you've got to be really smart to see through it all. There are no dumb people down here," he added proudly. Then, pointing to the bundle beside me, he asked, "What do you have there?"

"Some memories…Glimpses of what I saw…This is only the beginning of my life; there's so much more to see and to learn," I said, trying to sound thoughtful. To change the subject, I asked, "Aren't you curious about what is beyond this meadow?"

"Ha!" Auntie laughed. "Curious, she says? You must be pumped full of those big-eyed ideas they spread thick to smother the young and kill the slightest flicker of joy. All they want is for you to push the wheels of change that grind you to dust and to be proud of it. You pay highly for such extravagant ideas, though. *What's beyond the meadow?*" She said in a mocking singsong tone. "And what good is curiosity if the stuff you are curious about doesn't help you to live?"

Avoiding her eyes, I looked up, and there was the stranger's face again. He threw a knotted rope down into the pit, and, pressing the bundle of memories under my arm, I grabbed the rope and started climbing up. Near the top, the stranger helped me out of the pit, and I thanked him for coming back. While Jimmy and Auntie were clambering up, I asked, "Do you also live underground?"

"No, not me. I comb the grass that covers up the misery of the hopeless."

"Hopeless? You mean no one gets out of here?"

"I wouldn't say never, but very few people ever make up their minds to do so. They like it here."

I looked around, but neither Jimmy nor Auntie was to be seen.

"Don't mind them," said the keeper. "They must have jumped into some other pit already. The meadow is full of people like them, always in need of someone to wisecrack with. Commiseration nurtures their gloom and justifies their own misery."

"And what keeps you here?"

"I assist those who want to leave. I make myself useful. That is more than I could master anywhere else. I have no time to dwell on the bad parts of life. It's like scratching the wound that itches to be scratched. It never heals."

Hearing this, I pressed the bundle of memories tightly to my chest and felt it stir. Not all was lost.

"And how do you find your way in this meadow?" I asked him. "How do you avoid falling into these pits?"

"I place one foot in front of the other—like this—and before I shift my weight to the next step, I test the ground with my toe—like that—and if the ground feels firm, I shift my weight to the forward-pointing foot, and do this step after step. Once you get the hang of it, you have all the sky to enjoy and the luscious green and the lark that greets you every morning. Having this sunny meadow to myself and these unfortunate ones to take care of, what else could I wish for?"

Whistling a jolly tune and dancing his funny step-by-step, the keeper led me across the meadow. Imitating his gait, I followed, stopping here and there to explore a pit and to pass on what I had learned. And when I saw dirt flying up and falling back in, I'd stop to talk to the desperate digger, but they wouldn't hear what I had to say. And though my confidence in people and in life itself was shaken, I had the bundle of memories to hold on to.

4

In Clock Time

After seeing what people do to each other in the River of Time, it felt strange to be back home where life went on as usual. Yet nothing was the same.

The other day, after coming home from school, I went up to my room and could hardly believe my eyes—how messy it was! The bed had gone unmade for days, worn socks and tops were all over the place, and books and papers were piled on the desk collecting dust. I started cleaning up the mess—picked up things off the floor, fluffed out the quilt, emptied the trash can, vacuumed the room, and worked late into the night setting things straight.

While I was running about, my head was spinning. Having had a glimpse of how much misery life could hold, I started counting my blessings. Then and there I decided to get a grip on what I had, and I had it pretty good—at home no one pushed me around or asked prying questions. Mom, seeing me run up and down the stairs, didn't say a word; she just kept on smiling to herself. I guess she'd expected something like this would happen and was glad to see her daughter come to her senses.

"Taking charge of your life!" a harsh squawking voice made me turn. Perched on the windowsill was a red parrot, its head bobbing.

"That's right. You'll see!" I said, irritated by the intrusion.

"Planning ahead!" jabbered the parrot, as if it were making fun of me.

"I don't intend to wind up in the backwaters or the pits of life, bruised to bare bone!"

The parrot chuckled, "Well…That's to be seen!"

"Oh, leave me alone!"

It was late when I finished cleaning my room and climbed into bed. But I couldn't sleep. Thoughts were jostling—from what I just did to what I could have done better—and raking from one side of the brain to the other, finding no rest. Then, out of nowhere, the idea that no two events happen in the same place at the same time jabbed me hard—the logic couldn't be simpler: if I crammed my days with activities that would help me get ahead, the bad things would have no room, no place in which to happen!

From then on, time was a free commodity, like air or light. All I had to do was rely on my wits and use every minute to my advantage. With that as my rule, I set off each morning with new determination.

I soon learned that clock time was flexible. I could slow down time by moving slower and rush the passage of time by moving faster. It boiled down to this—by changing the speed of my own activities, I could make time, lose time, make up for lost time, and spend the left over time as I pleased. No wonder people were selling their time and buying time so others would do their work. In no time I was ready to invest (invest!) my time in projects that would improve my chances of getting the most out of whatever a situation had to offer.

If I studied harder, I'd have a good shot at going to a great college where I could study whatever I wished. Hearing that colleges liked well-rounded candidates, I went out for the basketball team, joined the debating team, and ran for class president. Finally I had a plan—something to aim for, to build a future on. I felt I could accomplish anything I set my mind to, and there was no one to stop me. The grown-ups, seeing how eager I was to excel, encouraged me and gave me advice at every turn; and riding on waves of good will, I could see my own future taking shape, all for the taking. How could I sit still?

At the peak of this heady excitement, after studying several hours for a history test, I fell asleep on my bed surrounded by books. I dreamt that I was in a room where the light was so bright that I could hardly see anything. Squinting, I made out pencil-thin outlines of boxes stacked high and wide; the place was too crammed to take a step in any direction. But when I tried to move a box out of the way, there was nothing but air—the outlines had no substance, the boxes were empty of content. I tried again, but every box I touched only cast a dark shadow—sharp-edged shadows leaving solid impressions. Picking up shadows instead of boxes, I stacked them on one side, and, noticing that the jagged edges interlocked like pieces of a huge puzzle, I started building intricate shadow constructions, delighting in the work and improving as I went along.

Flushed with excitement, I worked faster and faster, marveling at the ingenious shapes I created. Shapes seemed to generate themselves, as structures leaning toward each other interlocked, creating ever larger, more fabulous wholes. When I looked back to see how far I had come, I was startled to see a billy goat standing on its hind legs behind me, notepad in hand, its elegant coat gray-blue, its horns and hoofs polished black, the trimmed beard and eyelashes bleached snow-white.

"Go on, go on! Don't waste your time staring at me, you have much to ca-a-atch up with," he said in an edgy, high-pitched voice, adjusting the heavy blinders he wore to avoid distraction.

I looked up to see what I had to catch up with and saw on the horizon small and large stone circles, their shadows tracking the voyaging sun. In their shadow grew stone and mud brick huts and walls and towers. Also in their shadow rose dwellings that clustered into towns and cities and pyramids of all sizes to bring humanity closer to heaven and the mysteries of life. Out of their shadow grew the unfinished Tower of Babel, built for speaking to gods, and the Hanging Gardens of Babylon, cultivated to contemplate the sea of longings, and the Lighthouse of Alexandria, constructed to light the way. And out of their shadows—cast long and wide—grew temples and cathedrals—every shadow generating ever more elaborate longings that raised human aspirations higher. And though the longings themselves grew out of shadows, out of their ruin and rubble emerged the spectacle of sprawling modern cities—increasingly taller buildings crowding the sky, forever reaching for the high mysteries stacked ever higher and ever farther away.

I turned to the billy goat, scribbling in his notebook. "What are we looking at?"

"Civilizations built out of the sha-a-adows of previous civilizations, with the invincible ingenuity of humankind," he said, one eye twitching as if he had a tic.

"What are you writing?"

"I'm taking notes of what materials and how much of them were moved by people to build their dreams. So fa-a-a-ar it comes to seven trillion tons of stone, ninety-eight billion tons of rubble, two continents stripped of wood, three cross-continent ranges stripped of minerals, and four-fifths of the earth's deposits to fuel these ventures. Scientists are trying to figure out how long the riches of this planet will last."

"And then what?"

The billy goat scratched its side. "Everything will be reused; the civilizations following ours will be forced to recycle every scrap of material used so fa-a-ar."

While the billy goat was talking, the heap of shadow buildings kept growing, along with the din of hammering, chiseling, cutting, the sound of wheels squeaking, and the grind of machinery straining the air. Towering skyscrapers shot up, piercing the clouds, and in this grand extravaganza of glitter, a shiny metal arch brought back to earth a piece of sky. To the east and west of this heap were more towers and more temples and more pyramids, roofs with turned-up corners crowned misty mountaintops, and domed stone edifices squatted in manicured jungles. The world was overrun by the handiwork of people who had busied themselves—ever since it was discovered that shadows interlock and fit together into new wholes without apparent effort. All it took was the will to build and see a thought take shape, and nothing else mattered. Topping the heap were shiny rockets aimed at penetrating the heavens, and spaceships calmly glided above the protective outer layer, like insects adrift in thermals, probing ever farther into the deepening darkness of the universe. Slow-stirring distant nebulae transported vision into receding questions, while the already unraveled patterns baited the mind—the spectacle enacting the dance of life on the grandest of scales.

Disturbed by an ever-increasing commotion, I looked at the billy goat. He was taking notes at a furious speed, half of his face convulsing with an uncontrollable tic.

"I guess we too are contributing to the to-be-recycled heap of civilization?"

"Of course we a-a-are, every generation contributes its sha a-a-are of interpretations," said the billy goat. "Such is human nature, a-a-and who would want to restrain it? We are all in it together."

"We all?" I wondered.

"Yes, you and I as well. I supply the stubbornness necessary to accomplish anything worthwhile. I ma-a-a-ake people dream tall dreams and think big, which pushes humanity into the future. What you are looking at has been mostly achieved by the use of clocks—clocks synchronizing labor, clocks harnessing the human potential for the good of all. I suggest that you stop questioning everything you see, forget the eternal questions that ha-a-ave no answers, and do what is expected of every human being—share the responsibility for building a better tomorrow. Everyone will profit by it."

"Questions that have no answers—you mean, like 'What's the point of it all?'

He frowned. "It's beyond me-e-e why anyone would waste time on thoughts that flow like water down the drain. So much precious human potential is wa-a-asted on musings that invent problems rather than solve them and do more harm than good—that to this day I wonder what blinds so many people so consistently. On the other hand, everyone who devotes him or herself to what ma-a-a-atters to society and contributes to the good of all, joins the ra-a-a-anks of those who work for the future of humankind. Reliance on reason is the most productive way to spend one's life. And those who do so a-a-are the people on whose back civilization rests. Only those who grasp this are truly unselfish. The rest are dreamers living off wha-a-a-at these brave, self-denying people produce. Do not fall into this trap." By now his face was distorted by convulsions.

I asked, "Are you all right?" The billy goat nodded impatiently and I continued, "What about our personal dreams, hopes, and expectations?"

"What ma-a-a-akes you think that the things you see before you did not take imagination or dreams to guide the builders? Does it look to you as if these ingenious people were short of hope or expectation? They ha-a-a-ave used their lives productively and ha-a-ave directed their aspirations toward a common goal; they have given their lives to humanity. See what's been accomplished already, and you will understand what I mean."

"But aren't they building on shadows, with shadows?" I insisted.

He stomped his foot. "And what is a shadow, if not an indication that something is there to ca-a-ast a shadow? We distinguish things from one another only because there is light and shadow, and what you call day and night, or time, is also born of shadows cast by three planetary bodies in orbit. Somebody should write a book on the importance of shadows."

"Time, a shadow?" I ventured timidly.

"It's confusing, I know. Look—" and to demonstrate, the billy goat picked up the shadow of a box, as if it were cut out of paper, and lifting it up, slowly pressed it to the side of the box. The shadow vanished on contact.

"Now watch me do it fast." He lifted the shadow swiftly, and it vanished in a blink.

"The duration of the vanishing act you just witnessed corresponds to the speed of the movement. Whether short or long, any noticeable duration evokes the experience of time. No space, no motion; no motion, no duration; no duration, no perception of time. The word *time* merely stands in for the experience of the duration."

He took a deep breath. "Space, motion, and duration are components of everyday reality, grasped by the senses of people around the world." He paused again. "Once people noticed that the durations of night and day, the moon cycles, and cycles of the seasons corresponded with the movements of three planetary bodies, they started marking the movements, and so drew up a calendar. Only think about it—because people have observed these celestial shadows century after century, time was trapped in calendars and clocks! And once they had a calendar, the major cyclic events could be predicted and prepared for; the calendar not only punctuated the flow of time but also regulated every significant human activity and social event. By now calendars and clocks regulate even your personal life. Imagine—the notion of time, derived from the interactions of three rotating heavenly bodies, has set the rate at which time itself is supposed to flow!"

"Is there time in nature?" I ventured to interfere.

"In nature there's only duration, an immense variety of short and long durations that evoke the experience of time. It's the word 'time'—a name given to the experience, a mental conception—which raises questions, for the word stands in for all the durations, from nano seconds to light years. Thus our time standards, based on the movements of three celestial bodies, bypass the whole extent of durations that have gone on uninterrupted since the beginning of the world. When we use the standard time measures to account for periods of time, we are accounting not for the so-called passage of time, but merely the number of revolutions the sun has completed in that "stretch of time". Yet to this day all durations affect our being, as the velocity of our own inner states may clash or be in harmony with the dynamics prevalent in the surroundings. Hence, the many experiences of time.

Taking a deep breath and pointing at the achievements spread before us, the billy goat underscored the importance of his words with a grand sweeping gesture, "Just look where human ingenuity and daring have ta-a-a-aken us already! All due to clocks and a constructive use of time!"

Having difficulty following what he said, I envisioned masses of people felling forests, quarrying stone, building walls, towers, houses, bridges, castles, cities, and temples; repairing or tearing down old buildings and building new ones in their place; moving tons of materials from one place to another and back; and rushing blindly into a programmed future as if there were no tomorrow.

"But the people—they are like ants…"

The billy goat adjusted his blinders. "Everything has its price." An attack of tics made him pause. "No exceptions here, but the rewards a-a-are immense. First of all, never forget that these ant-like people supply you with a-a-all your needs. Be it in technology, science, medicine, or anything else on the market today, their persistence and perseverance have given humanity the building blocks of knowledge. It's mind boggling how fa-a-a-ar better-off people are today than they were only a few generations ago. If that is not proof of progress, well then…" Seeing me suppress a yawn, he cleared his throat. "I've said enough."

"And to whom are we proving what?"

He threw up his forelegs. "Look at it this way...Whatever the undertaking, progress is the feeling of going forward in a direction. Progress is witness to our infallible ingenuity. And progress gives hope because it carries a promise for a better future. Humanity needs hope, something to look forward to, to move on. But enough...I have work to do." He said, disappointment in his voice.

"I may not understand what you said, but please go on." Feeling that I had let him down, I had to say something. Then I added politely, "Having come this far to find out what life is about, I want to see it all."

Looking away, the billy goat spoke reluctantly, "What I am trying to say is that the ra-a-ational outlook, the ra-ational approach, and the ra-ational frame of mind are the most constructive and the least wasteful of all possible outlooks. People are not called Homo sapiens for nothing, so why not harness the mind to its intended purpose? Securing a better tomorrow for humankind is the ultimate challenge, and sooner or la-a-a-ater scientists will find the answers to what plagues humanity today. The present is only a means of getting there."

"Its intended purpose? Intended by whom? And the present is only a means? Don't we do our living and seeing and thinking in the present? Or can living too be switched on and off at will?" I stepped back, alarmed by what I said.

"What kind of living do you have in mind, young lady?"

"That's what I want to find out, that's why I'm here—to see what options I have."

In a voice, now harsh and raspy, he said, "Regardless of how you choose to spend your life, there will always be difficulties to bear, things to complain about, and things to wish for." Catching himself, he added, "But I've talked too much already. By the way, if you plan to go on, you better finish what you've started, or it will come back to haunt you."

With these words, the billy goat turned away. Notebook in hand, pencil at the ready, he stepped into the world of shadows.

I shouted after him, "And what about the present?"

"What other present is there?" his voice came back.

"And the future?"

"The future is but one other event in the ma-a-a-aking!" His voice was fading.

"Well, I want it all," I shouted back. And heard nothing.

Compelled to continue the work where I'd left off—compelled by whom? The billy goat, society, the time machine?—I was so steamed up that when I turned to finish the work I had started, I built ever larger and more outrageous shadow constructions. When I paused to catch my breath and see what I'd accomplished, I was impressed—shapes evolved one from the other, and as they grew in scope and complexity, they complemented each other, extending the possibilities in many directions. Progress was evident in every structure, the process immensely gratifying. Only one structure struck me as somewhat peculiar. It resembled an ancient observatory made entirely of steps going up and down, steps diminishing in every direction, as if seen in multiple mirror reflections.

I approached the structure slowly and, after walking around it several times, touched it to see whether it was real. As if shocked, the shadow structure swayed, then cracked, then started crumbling. It crumbled so slowly, so silently, and in such an otherworldly way, that dumbstruck, I stood there watching my fancy handiwork self-destruct. And as if this elaborate likeness of a real thing were the epi-center of an earthquake, shockwaves rippled the ground, and wave-by-wave all the structures splintered and shattered, collapsing into dust. Struck more by the eerie silence than by the destruction, I real-ized that I had misused that precious commodity called time—in the frenzy of invention, fascinated by how my busy hands held the mind captive, I wasted my time on making things that were utterly meaningless to me.

As I watched the shockwaves recede, and I faced the emptiness I myself had created, I saw no boundaries, no horizon, and no limita-tions—only waves of aftershock rippling my starved brain.

Faint voices made me turn around. Not far from where I stood, perched on an outcropping of boulders were the white sparrow, the red parrot, a raven, a barn owl, and a white crane.

The white sparrow was speaking. "I'll repeat, I have called this meeting not to discuss whether the girl is ready to continue on this voyage, but whether we should give her a break and stop her from going ahead."

"She hasn't hit the wall yet, has she?" asked the crane, glancing at the raven.

"I'd rather see her get the full measure of every facet of time, or the next facet will make no sense to a girl who plunges head on into every situation," said the black raven, its voice insistent.

"So far, we have seen little hesitation or fear." Added the owl.

"I'd show no mercy to anyone who got that far already, for only those who pass the test of endurance are apt to reach the end," said the crane, not mincing words.

"Though all keep dreaming of it," interjected the parrot.

"Then it's settled," said the owl. "And let's not forget that like everyone else, she has a second chance. As young as she is, she may not make it to the end this time, but she may come back later, stronger and more persistent, ready to experience the full range of options without a hitch."

"Yes," agreed the white sparrow, "but the girl does not know that. And as headstrong as she is, we don't want her to crash too hard."

"There is no such thing as crashing too hard. Those willing to grow welcome every challenge and grow stronger for it," said the raven.

"True," responded the owl, humming its favorite tune. "It's what you do with what you've got, and never mind how much you got…" Showered with glances, she quieted down.

"So it's agreed then, we shall not spare Alya. She is to experience all the pressures, stresses, dangers, and delights allotted to every curious and daring person," concluded the white sparrow.

"Aye, aye…" resounded the birds in unison and took off, each in a different direction.

The edge of something hard against my shoulder made me turn in bed. It was the history book, and the bedside light was still on. Seeing that I'd fallen asleep fully dressed, I got up, put the books on the table, put on my pajamas, and crawled back into bed. But I could not sleep. What the birds had said sounded not only grim but also dangerous, surely not encouraging. I gathered that I had stepped onto some ancient path, still familiar to birds but forgotten by people. On the other hand, what the birds said about me gave me confidence that I was able to handle what lay ahead.

While musing about the mysterious ways of life, I was struck by how, in human affairs, every step had to be planned and every detail had to be carefully attended to and scrupulously supervised, or an event set in motion might come to a standstill or take an unpredictable turn or run amuck to a disastrous ending. This led to another chilling thought; namely, that in events initiated by people, every step had to be accounted for; that every intentional human act was a link in a chain of right or wrong actions registered as a black or red entry in the balance sheets of gains and losses. Someone was responsible for each good and bad outcome; someone had contributed to the way things turned out in the end.

I had taken control of my life all right, and there was no one to stop me. To the contrary, all I heard these days at home and in school was praises for my cheerful disposition and unwavering commitment. Proud of myself, I finally dozed off.

5

In Listless Time

For the last few weeks, I had been feeling out of sorts. It had started when Mom got sick, which happened just before spring break, when instead of taking the trip we had planned for months, she had to be hospitalized. I cooked and cleaned the house, and although Mom was recovering after her operation, this unexpected turn of events shook me up. What if Dad fell sick too, or worse? What if a tornado struck our house, as had happened to my cousins in Kansas? I had heard enough about disasters to know that sweeping events can destroy the most carefully planned human arrangements. It was foolish to think that I was in control of my life.

Before her sickness, the world felt solid underfoot. Now, seeing how fragile and fickle life could be, that solid ground had broken up again—every creature small and big, every blade of grass and speck of dust, every star and planet was spinning toward its own separate annihilation to be determined by a million little turns and twists.

Nothing made sense anymore. Why was I pushing myself so hard, what was the rush? Where to? What was the fuss and bustle all about if it only led to more of the same? Why suffer if every expectation was stained with pain, and every success was marred by its own specific frustration? In the end, what difference did it make how I amused myself year after year?

The confident self I had been was but an echo in my mind, an idea left over from the past, adrift somewhere and useless now. Every morning I made breakfast and brought a tray to Mom. Every morning Dad went to work; I went to school. And after school, I rushed home to do what was expected of me. The routine was boring, but I had no bad feelings about it.

Mom was recovering as expected, and the end to this drudgery was in sight. But I had withdrawn so deep into myself that I hardly heard what was said when someone was speaking, and when I spoke, no one seemed to listen. The sense of isolation followed me outside the house. My feet were taking me to school or to the store; my feet remembered the way from one street to another, but my head was set on a different course.

I didn't think much about it. Isolation made me unreachable and inaccessible to others, and that gave me much comfort. Yet soon I was no longer able to respond to people even if I wanted to. One afternoon, as I walked in from school, Mom turned to me and hugged me tightly. In a sudden rush of emotion, I wanted to hug her back but restrained myself, because it felt like a weakening of will. The other night Dad suggested that we go to the movies, but instead of saying something, I just sat there listless, looking at him. He brought my jacket, helped me put it on, and took me by the hand to the car. I can't say I didn't enjoy going out or seeing the movie. It simply made no difference where I was, or what was going on around me.

Silence offered protection from the pressures without and within. Silence gave me a much-needed vacation from dealing with the world. And as silence enveloped me like a cocoon, after much twisting inside, the cocoon felt warm against my skin. Drum-tight around me, it fit me better than my shadow. There was no need to change anything.

Though my hectic schedule had subsided, in school I was still sitting on needles, still trying to fade out of sight. Was there anyone, anything in the world I could trust again?

A shadow squatting atop the cocoon cawed, "You can trust time. Time is on your side."

"Who are you?"

"I'm the raven from Nevermore. You're in my domain now." Not knowing what to say, I kept silent. "Stop peering into a midnight dreary," said the raven, echoing Edgar Allan Poe.

Hadn't time brought me to this? Maybe the raven was right—maybe time did carry a promise of change. So all I had to do was sit and wait. But to do nothing wasn't that easy, for flashes of an active self disturbed the present, while being idle undermined the future. I was sure of that. And as I waited for something significant to happen, time on my hands grew heavy like a stone carried uphill. With hope swaddled in ridicule, the deadweight of time—listless and stagnant—was crushing every budding thought.

One by one, glimpses of familiar faces and snippets of past events came to mind as if to bid me farewell. Gathered in the corner of my mind, images acted out a scene and replaced thought; words surfaced rarely, like subtitles in silent movies. As in a silent film, generation after generation of ancestors aligned to the left of me: the procession receded into the far recesses of time, the unbroken line telescoping beyond the horizon. And on my right my future was unfolding—tomorrow still in the cocoon; a year from now in some other place and state of mind, two years later in college—yes. Then maybe a job, marriage, and children—yes. Then my children are having children, then the solemn procession of births and funerals—all the inevitable *yeses* that string together in a human life. As humanity proceeded into the future—I was but a speck in the chain—somewhere beyond the horizon, the past and the future touched. In a flash, the circle closed and fused. Rocked by seismic waves, with a shudder I woke to the present.

The cocoon felt so tight I could hardly move a limb. A tapping made me look up.

"You there, still wallowing in self-pity? Speak up!" I heard the raven's raspy voice. Detecting a sinister note, I didn't feel like talking. When I looked up, I met the raven's black eye pressed against a hole in the shell, staring at me.

"Would you rather be dead than alive?"

"I was sleeping when your tapping woke me up, and…" Suddenly, shocked by the question, I started to mumble.

"And? What were you going to say?" he insisted, his black beak widening the breathing hole, pecking at the edges of my melancholy.

"I'm waiting for time to bring change. Nothing more…"

"Did I hear you right? Did you say you are waiting for change to come to you?"

"Yes."

"Changes have taken place around you the whole time you were sulking, and you're waiting for something special to be delivered, especially for you? Don't you know that all things change as they must, and that includes your precious self?"

"What changes?" I had to know.

"For one, the cocoon has grown so thick that by now you are trapped inside it."

"Trapped?" Suddenly breathing became difficult. I cried out, "How much longer will this last?"

The raven perching above the breathing hole was silent.

I tried again. "Is the end near?"

But the raven spoke no more. Yet the thought that there must be an end to this made a U-turn in my mind. Didn't I have the *yeses* to look forward to? Now the slightest inkling of change felt like the promise of a spectacular escape—change the savior, change the redeeming force that was to rescue me from a pending disaster—

Gasping for air, I twisted and pushed hard against the breathing hole, and my head popped out into a jet-black night. I heard what sounded like a distant wind, but then it changed, like water falling down a chasm. And then a flood wave hit the cocoon. With only my head sticking out, the cocoon bobbed and tilted from side to side, taking on water; water sloshed inside the cocoon making ominous sounds. The contraption was set on its own predestined course.

Now the futility of human arrangements struck me hard: Wasn't I trapped in a shell of my own making? Hadn't I built the cocoon to protect myself from the outside world? Hadn't my wish for isolation imprisoned me? At daybreak the cocoon was already half full of water and tilting precariously. There was no land in sight, only huge, lazy waves rolling one after the other, carrying me out to sea.

"Get out!" A seagull shrieked above my head. Seeing my upturned face full of questions, the bird screeched into my ear, "Stop thinking! Act!"

Pushing at the opening as hard as I could, I popped out of the cocoon just in time—wobbling this way and that way, it sank. A few bubbles of air rose to the surface; then there was nothing left for me to hold on to.

Freezing, I swam quickly, looking neither back nor ahead. When a monumental wave about to crest overtook me, it lifted me higher and higher, and I glimpsed a dark stretch of land—the wave was about to break on the black rocks lining the shore. I shut my eyes, but there was no crash; for before reaching shore, the wave subsided to a gentle roll, and I washed up on a narrow stretch of sand. Greatly relieved, I stood up tall and started walking along the towering cliffs.

Some distance ahead the cliffs jutted out close to water, and there I noticed a flicker of flame. As I approached it, through a narrow slit in the rock, I could see a fire burning but not much more. Trying to squeeze in, I stuck my leg into the slit but stopped short. On the other side, a group of people were huddled around a fire over which a cauldron, full of a thick liquid, was bubbling; the sweet aroma of honey was heavy in the air. Those close to the cauldron held long-handled spoons or large wooden ladles, while those standing behind them held sticks. Eagerly they dipped their implements into the hot honey and then anointed themselves with it. Those who had spoons or ladles poured the steaming goo over their heads, scorching their ears and faces and blistering their shoulders. Woeful, suppressed moans filled the cave. Yet no matter how painfully scorched they were, none could resist the taste of honey—they greedily licked it off their hands and bodies, as if the self-inflicted pain were worth the suffering, as if the addiction were justifiable.

Nauseated by what I saw and alarmed by vaguely familiar echoes of self-mutilation, I slipped back unnoticed. Sobbing uncontrollably, I ran along the cliffs until I came upon a tongue of sand stretching inland. Glad to leave the beach, I turned up the path between the tall, jagged rocks and hadn't gone far when the narrow path forked. Without a thought, I turned left. But a few yards later I stopped, no longer sure whether I had taken the right turn. In hesitation I walked back and forth, entered the right fork, returned to the left, and, sickened by indecision, I looked up. On the right, where the path turned, were steps hewn in stone leading to the top of the cliff.

The climb was steep and treacherous; the narrow steps were crumbling underfoot. I was not alone—my shadow, a fiery red, was walking beside me, flames cresting like plumes atop its head. With every step I took, tongues of fire licked the face of the cliff. When I stopped, my shadow climbed on, and, upon reaching the top of the cliff, like a ball of fire, it rolled out of sight.

At the top of the steps lay a burned out sun-drenched plateau. Utterly alone, I didn't want to cross it, and, seeing treetops above a cluster of boulders farther up the edge, to escape the scorching sun, I headed in its direction.

There, in a silvery shade, an old man was planning wood, his unhurried motions showing that he'd been long at the task. I said hello, but the carpenter neither looked up nor spoke. Knee-deep in shavings, both the man and the wood cast a sharp metallic sheen. But unlike the carpenter's curls, which fell loosely on his forehead, the silvery shavings coiled fiercely compact.

"What are you building?" I ventured to ask.

Without lifting his head he answered, "I build ships—like promises of events to come."

"And who might be using these ships?"

"Those who trust the wind," he said.

Sensing that I had outstayed my welcome, I said goodbye and left. Outside the cluster of boulders, I looked over the rim of the cliffs. In the waters below, a ship was setting out to sea; the ship was built to withstand raging waters, sails rigged for a distant voyage.

6

In Personal Time

Home in time for supper, I found a visitor seated at the table, a distant cousin of my father's. I don't remember meeting Uncle Jack before, but I had heard about him—he was referred to as the black sheep of the family. He sat erect in his chair, his body wiry and tense, a faded jacket hanging on his shoulders. The well-trimmed mustache under his delicate nose made him look foreign.

Mom and Dad seemed delighted to see the much-talked about drifter. We lingered at the table long after dessert was finished and listened to stories of his travels in faraway lands and unheard-of countries.

During a pause I asked him, "How do you know what turn to take, where to go next?"

He smiled. "It's simple. Once you get the hang of it, there's nothing to it. Let's say I'm on the coast of Africa feeling homesick. A week or so later, while having breakfast in a joint up the street, I hear a guy say that last night a ship, en route to the States, has docked in the harbor. I go to the harbor, find the ship's captain, and tell him I want to go home but have no money for a ticket. He tells me to show up at six on Tuesday morning and gives me a job. Off we sail, and here I am."

He shrugged his shoulders. "All I had to do was know where I wanted to be next, then keep my ears and eyes open. With ears cocked to hear specific things and eyes on the lookout, I picked up what I needed to hear or see. Before I began feeling homesick, people would talk about ships bound for the States every other day. And it had no effect on me, because I'd say to myself, 'So what, let them come and go, they have nothing to do with me.' But not this time. This time it struck the bull's-eye. Don't things like this happen to you?"

"I think so. A few months ago my teacher was talking about deserts. I wanted to learn more about the people who spend their lives in such a hostile environment, and on my next visit to the library, on the librarian's desk, *The People of the Kalahari Desert* was staring up at me. Is that what you mean?"

"Exactly. Of course, wanting comes first—it fixates your attention on specific things. And by wanting, I don't mean wishing for things that money could buy. It's wishing for changes in your life that will take you out of one situation and place you in another." He leaned back in his chair. "And for that you need to listen to your innermost self and also observe what is going on in your surroundings. When the two converge, it's like a lightning bolt has struck you, and you know the time has come to act—to take the chance which offers itself and so make change happen. You've simply got to listen to what your inner self is saying."

Dad shifted uneasily in his chair. "Jack, don't you think that the heart can be misleading, especially for the young?"

Sitting up straight again, Uncle Jack continued. "The yearnings I'm talking about are not rooted in the heart, which is finicky and apt to change from moment to moment. They spring from the quick of your being, from the soul or the spirit, or whatever you call it. Actually, it doesn't feel like wishing, but more like anticipating for something to happen—like a premonition hanging in the air. And you know, it's not frivolous when this deep unrest begins to cast a shadow on your daily activities. That's how you know it's time to move on, to change either your surroundings or your frame of mind. If you wait and do nothing, by choosing to ignore that internal urge, you invite more dangerous changes than those your spirit urges you to make."

Flashes of me in the cocoon swirled through my mind. Uncle Jack was looking at me. "A true yearning pulls you toward thoughts or actions that renew your sense of self—make more of you, not less; give hope; incite; push you on."

Now I understood. Shutting out the world, as I did by spinning a cocoon, did not make more of me. Isolation made me shrink and shrivel, and that was the opposite of what my Uncle was talking about.

Uncle Jack's eyes remained on me. He looked deadly serious. "Though most people tend to ignore these deep-rooted longings, they never really go away but gnaw silently at the core of your being. Some may even haunt you for the rest of your life."

A silence settled over the table. Somewhat hesitantly, Mom asked, "And are you happy, Jack, about where this kind of life has taken you?"

Playing with his fork, Uncle Jack answered softly, "Looking back on it all, I have to say no, not really. As you know, I wasn't fit to hold a nine-to-five job. Not all of us are. But where I failed, really failed, is that I never found an objective or had a dream to guide me—something that would validate all my wanderings. Some kind of a scholarly pursuit could have done it, or an exploration of sorts could have taken me to certain places to gather specific information.

And if the pursuit proved to be worthwhile, I could share it with others—write a paper, publish a book. I traveled in search of something, but I never gave enough thought to what it was I was really searching for. I guess I was hoping to stumble upon it—actually expecting for that dream or vision to come and hit me in the face."

Looking straight at me, Uncle Jack added: "You must do better than that, Alya. Start forming a vision of yourself doing something exciting in the future. The vision doesn't have to be all that grand. It only has to spark your curiosity and lead you from one point in life to another." A faint smile washed over his face. "That I did not have."

Mom had been listening to Uncle Jack with a distant look in her eyes. "Not everyone is fit for that kind of life either," she said. Then she turned to look at me and seeing how attentively I listened, said firmly. "It's getting late, Alya. Uncle Jack is staying with us for a whole week, there will be plenty of time to talk about things."

At the door I turned and asked my uncle, "Is it too late for you to have a vision?"

After a long silence, he finally looked up and said, "Maybe that's why I came back—to find out."

Climbing the steps to my room, I grasped what Uncle Jack was talking about—not of the world out there, not of the rational world, but about that very personal world we call our own, where we make sense of it all. So the mind was also divided, part rational and part irrational. And why was the irrational made up of dreams and all sorts of unexplainable urges, constantly baffling the rational mind? Did dreams have a logic different from the linear logic of cause and effect on which reasoning depended? If so, what was this logic? Where would one look for it?

That night I dreamt that I was walking along a path across a meadow, a shortcut home I often took. Halfway along the path I felt an urge to look back. Seeing nothing in particular, I walked on. The urge, however, persisted, and before leaving the meadow, I had to look back once more. Now in the middle of the meadow stood a blue door with three white steps leading up to it. I walked back to the door, climbed the three steps, and knocked. The door opened a crack, and a hand holding a blue lollypop reached out. I took the lollypop, the hand withdrew, and the door shut tight again. Curious to see who was so generous, I knocked and knocked again, but no one answered. Walking around the door and seeing that it lead nowhere, I opened it.

Behind it lay an empty chalk-white room with another door on the opposite wall. I crossed the room and without knocking opened that door as well. Behind it was another empty white room, only smaller in size, my head almost touching the ceiling. Feeling crammed already, I thought I'd better go back; but when I turned around, the door I had just passed through was no longer there. So I opened the door in front of me and found a smaller room and then a smaller room still. I was already crouching when I crawled into a room so small that I could hardly move. A doorknob was pressing against my shoulder, and when I reached for it, a door behind me sprung open. Like a contortionist, I pushed myself limb by limb through the small opening, and when I finally emerged on the other side of this obstacle course and stood up, I was ankle-deep in a sunset-pink cloud.

Drumbeats underfoot prompted me to stand still. And as I stood, inches away from me, a bold head pushed up; then the shoulders, back, and buttocks jerked upward as if the person were climbing steps inside the cloud—man or woman I could not tell. Suddenly cloud-dwellers were everywhere, walking as if on different levels fixed below the misty surface—heads bobbing here, torsos swaying there, others wading knee deep. All the heads were bald, all the faces were pallid and expressionless, all were wearing identical tunics the color of the cloud, and all were moving in step to the thumping beat underfoot.

I asked a passing cloud-dweller, "What do you people call yourselves?" Somnambulant faces turned in my direction as if searching for the source of the sound.

"What's the name of this place?" I inquired again, but the cloud dwellers merely looked at each other as if they were hearing a foreign tongue.

"Where am I?" I insisted.

Now they all started talking at once in a language I didn't recognize and pointing at the sun, the moon, and me standing among them—as if I were part of some celestial triangulation or held the answer to their misplaced or misbegotten lives, which were stuck on some interim, dreamy level of existence from which they wished to escape. But how could I point out a direction if I had no idea where I was? I had only a wish to find the door behind which living seemed as effortless as breathing.

A muffled, cloud-locked voice echoed in the air.

"Here the laws of attraction will guide you. When your heartbeat quickens, trust whatever offers itself to you, and it will take you where you want to go."

By then the inhabitants of the cloud were swarming around me, and in a swirl of confusion, I was sucked under.

Falling through layers of clouds, I landed softly in some deep underground passage; the light was so dim that it took awhile for my eyes to get used to it. What I saw was not encouraging: on the right and the left of me the walls were lined with doors, all shut. Most of the doors were marked with strange signs—some had deep scratch-marks on them, some were stained with blood-red splashes, and others were bulging, as if the space behind them were stuffed to burst.

Noticing an unmarked door, I knocked three times. A man with a face of bark opened it a crack and looked at me. "Yes?" He asked in a small voice, as if talking were painful; his eyes, imbedded in the cracks of bark, were blinking fast.

"I'm looking for the door to a hidden chamber…" I blurted out.

"A hidden chamber? Never heard of it. Try the last door on the far right. The one who lives there might know of such arcane things."

I thanked him and walked over to the last door on the far right, the hollow echoes of my footsteps running ahead of me. I knocked twice on the door, and an old woman, overgrown with pale blue lichen, appeared in the doorway. I told her what I was looking for and she said, "Yes, there is such a chamber. But I've forgotten where it is or how to find it." Her voice was as soft as the whisper of wind rolling over a mossy stone. "Try the last door on your left. You might have better luck there," she said, shutting the door.

An elderly woman, a spindly shrub of hair on her head, opened the last door on the left. The few buds on her head were tipped shocking green and promised change. After hearing what I had to say, she pointed to the dark shadows down the corridor, and catching her breath she said, "You might—you just might—find a passage there."

I thanked her and entered the shadows.

Groping in the darkness, I climbed a steep and slippery incline, water dripping insistently, measuring the passage of time. And when at the end of the seemingly endless corridor I came to another closed door, grim forebodings invaded my mind. Heart pounding, I raised my hand to knock when the door swung open by itself.

A blast of white heat hit my face. Squinting I saw a radiant clock the size of a blazing sun suspended in midair, its many hands pointing in all directions—the short, upright ones were moving fast, and the long ones were grazing the outer peripheries of the clock's blank face. Some kind of a universal joint at the core rotated all the hands from left to right, and one timekeeper took care of all the movements at once. The clock was timing the duration of every event in my life, from start to finish: the short hand I was looking at was timing the healing of a cut in my finger, a longer hand was ticking away the time allotted to my schooling, the longest one, its point outside the clock's rim, was timing the span of my life. The monotonous hum of an event's duration was set to end after a hand completed a predetermined number of revolutions; the short hands wound up for hours, days, or weeks, while the longer ones ran for months and years. The glow was so intense that I had to turn away.

Not far from where I stood, a flock of white geese was feeding on the sun-bleached grass lining the banks of a reflective pond. I took a step forward, and the invisible clock chimed the hour of beginnings.

A startled goose lifted its head at the sound. Seeing me, she waddled over.

"I found the door; I've seen the clock!" I shouted excitedly.

The goose replied curiously, "You have? Then come with us!"

I followed the goose as if pulled by a magnet, and by the time I reached her, I was so small I could hardly see over her shoulders. She lowered her white wing to the ground, and climbing the feathers like rungs of a ladder, I sat down on her back, my legs dangling around her neck. With an outbreak of cackles, the flock took off in a *V*-formation, and I was carried away.

And what a delight it was to be in the air, to feel the wind in my face! I could see from up high the airy distances waiting for me—all directions favorable! The whole world was offering itself to me—all for the taking! I could hardly believe what a promising life laid before me! This is how life was to be lived! This is how I was to live from now on!

With my heart pounding, I leaned into the wind and shouted, "Take me down! I have no time for this!"

"Time is the password to change!" shrieked back the goose, slowly beating her wings.

Eager to plunge into my new life, I insisted. "Where are you taking me?"

"We're riding a current of changes, and that's what you need!" answered the goose. "Change in time will take you from point to turning point; each point will bring you closer to where you wish to be."

"How will I know which turn to take?"

"A host of sensations buzzing inside you will tell you. Trust what suggests itself to you."

We were flying over a range of snowcapped mountains, and feeling a chill, I buried myself in the goose's feathers. I must have dozed off, for when I looked down again, we were on the other side of the mountains. There, in a field of summer wheat, the flock descended. I thanked the goose for the ride, slipped off her back, and regained at once my normal size.

Close to where I stood, white cranes were dancing. Struck by the beauty of their courtship ritual, I stood still and watched them. A crane glanced over and, without interrupting its dance, asked in an air-splicing voice, "Can you dance?"

I blinked. "Not really…"

"Too bad, we could have taken you to heaven!"

"I've no time…" I started to explain.

"Then look for what's moving—moving away from where you are." Still dancing, step-by-step the crane moved closer. "Don't be fussy about the direction." It spread its wings and raised its head. "Hitch on to the nearest thing—the thing that moves." The crane made a slow turn, the tips of its wings brushing the ground. "Hitch-hiking will take you there."

"I must go back…" I said, anxious to start living in earnest, already envisioning and planning my new adventurous life. I had no patience to listen to what I was supposed to be doing next.

"In this time frame planning is futile; it invites frustration." With a hop the crane rose into the air, then descended, its wings slicing the air. "Toss a wish into the future, then listen to—listen to where it falls, and then trust whatever offers you a ride in that direction. Take the ride." After making a half turn and poking its beak in different directions, it continued. "The road is not straight—it will twist and turn, and if the vehicle starts slowing down or changes its course, look around again." Wings spread wide, legs dancing to a silent beat, the crane said, "Change will bring you there." Raising its head to the sky, it added, "There are no shortcuts here."

As I stood there mesmerized by the spectacle, it dawned on me that the doors I'd already opened were but a testing of my perseverance—whether I had the gumption to go on. Only now, after I'd found the clock that timed every instant of my life, only after seeing the wide-open distances, was I ready to take the unmapped, uncharted road paved by sensations. The sweet urge that brought me to this point was the taste of the lollipop. And I knew at once that failure to act—to trust what offered me a ride—would be a waste of the time allotted to me on earth. All that was missing was a vision flung far enough into the future to guide me. But that was to come. Animated to the brink of bursting, in a hurry to start living my own life for the first time, I was ready to run in any direction.

The sharp voice of the crane stopped me. "Rushing events? Impossible. In this personal—personal time zone, change is the vehicle, while time merely takes the measure of distances traveled."

"I must move on, my time is ticking away!" I said anxiously.

"Look around—see anything moving?"

A turtle was walking by. Drawn to it, I climbed onto its back, and as soon as it started walking, I regretted my choice of the turtle at once—if only it would go faster...if only I had looked around more...if only—

"You in a hurry?" asked the turtle in a low, misty voice that came across great distances.

"Very much so! There is so much to do!"

"I'm going as fast as I can," said the turtle, not increasing its pace. "Hold on...Hold yourself tight..."

The hypnotic tone and the slow-rolling waves of sound calmed me down. And ever so slowly, a vibrant, deep hum filled me with a delirious sense of wellbeing, as if in its ancient wisdom the sky itself was leaning over me and taking me under its lofty wing. And while the turtle took its time plodding onward, I tried to clear my head of the bickering noises that disturbed the calm.

As if reading my mind, the turtle spoke. "Runaway thoughts are like hurricane winds…Let them be, don't fight them. They'll spend themselves in due time. Nothing lasts forever."

"You mean doing nothing will help me stay the course?"

As if talking were useless, the turtle was silent for a while. Finally he answered, "Letting things be is not doing nothing. It's a decision that impels you to be not anxious but vigilant." His words sank into me like a handful of sun-warmed pebbles. "If you take the path that suggests itself, which is the path of least resistance, you will not be resigning passively but entering a flow—attuning to what otherwise might pass you by or throw you off course unnoticed." Pausing again, as if waiting for his words to sink in, he continued, "And though at times doing nothing may look slower, and sometimes it takes longer, you will waste neither time nor energy on frenzied activities and, without missing a beat, will reach your destination. The path of least resistance is paved by hope sprung fresh at every turn."

The turtle stopped so abruptly that I rolled off its back. By the time I stood up, it was nowhere to be seen.

Suddenly abandoned and alone under a tall, unfriendly sky, I looked around. There was nothing to see but a quicksilver streak on the faintly glowing horizon. The streak was pulsating—getting wider and taller—as if an ocean were rising. Rolling in my direction, the wall of water was gaining on me fast, already nine stories high, when in the heart of this towering menace, I saw a whirling, watery eye fixed on me. The wall was almost on top of me when, gripped by a will greater than mine, I stared back at it. My unblinking gaze shut out the watery eye, and the wall stopped in its tracks.

A high voice crossed the distance. Faint at first, it soon flooded the air with song. I looked up, and there, on top of the menacing wall, in the high cresting foam, was a huge drop of water bobbing on water. Illuminated by a hundred suns, it cast an eerie glow.

My heart leaped when the watery sphere started bouncing to the rhythm of the song, and when it reached the far edge of the water wall, against which a rainbow was leaning, the sphere slid down the majestic chute of colors. Bouncing away, it left a trail of flames behind it. The heavenly voice struck a note so high and pure that I took the sphere to be the essence of my being—that which kept the inner clock ticking. When the voice hit a still higher note, I ran after the sphere. And as soon as I stepped into the trail of flames, I caught on fire, and though flames danced over me, I did not burn. Whatever I touched on the run—a blade of grass, a drop of dew, a stone—I set them on fire, yet nothing was consumed.

I caught up with the sphere, and when I gathered it up in my arms, in the duration of a single high-pitched, triumphantly glorious note, it shrank to the size of a glowing, white pebble. I gasped, lest the sphere vanished all together, and that instant the pebble nestling in my palm leaped into my parted lips and I swallowed it. The song faded and the sunspot settled behind my breastbone. And with a singleness of purpose, it tugged—the tug familiar to birds in navigation.

With an overwhelming sense of freedom—every direction inviting, every door wide open—I met the world with my lungs shouting, "The shadows have lifted! The journey is neither dream nor tale!"

Listening to the internal clock bells chime jubilation, I breathed in all the freedom that my lungs could hold and drank up all the light that I could scoop up with my hands. And true to the nature of waves, the joy slowly ebbed away.

What I heard next was Mom's voice. "Wake up, Alya. It's time to get up!"

And I ebbed, returning to the world of words.

7

In Circular Time

In the fall of my junior year, once again without warning, I was drawn into another frame of mind. My days at school and at home were now like beads, strung on a spiraling loop of time.

On some days I was back where I'd been many times before—helping Mom clean the house and wash the dishes or helping Dad rake the lawn and wash the windows. Doing the same things year after year, I went through the same motions, sifting through the same thoughts over and over again. Small changes—a crack in a dish or a windowpane or an acorn rooting in the lawn—caused much excitement. On other days I'd get ahead of myself, with thoughts leaning into my future, and I entertained thoughts of what awaited me when I graduated from high school. Routine at home and routine in school—my personal world and the world outside—were running on parallel tracks.

Routine wove the cloth of my existence. Though all sorts of unexpected events were apt to upset the daily rhythm, activities at home and in school readily adjusted. But when the inner and outer worlds intersected or collided, as happened from time to time, changes had to be made and priorities had to be set. Quick orientation helped to decide what adjustments were needed to restore a functional daily routine.

Days came around like a recurrent dream. If in personal time the clock would tick until a duration reached its appointed hour, in a circular frame of mind, time flowed like sand in an hourglass—hours passing through the narrows of the present slipped from the past into the future hardly noticed. And when the sands of time ran out and the glass was turned over, the past carried over into the future. The hypnotic steadiness of days, tasks, and seasons—generation after generation unbroken—gave a sense of security: repetition made the world seem predictable and stable.

At home the routine seldom varied. Yet even at breakfast, neither Mom nor Dad was ever quite the same. Some mornings they exchanged furtive glances and talked hurriedly; at other times, faint smiles washed over their faces as if they shared a secret—an exchange of lingering glances showed them unwilling to part. I too was never quite the same. On some days I was eager to go to school, while on others I wished I could stay at home. I was never truly indifferent to the day ahead, for there was always something to look forward to or to dread.

Repetition was the key, yet numerous small events hinted of what was in the air. Mom had taken a part-time job at a nearby nursery, and upon entering the kitchen after school, I'd look to see if there were flowers on the table, a sure giveaway of the mood at dinner that evening. A cut geranium bloom or a few pansies in a small bud vase meant a simple meal, nothing out of the ordinary; a rose in the same vase meant Mom had something exciting to tell. Flowers saved from a larger bouquet spoke of leftovers to be served tonight. No flowers meant she was distracted with something weighing on her mind.

True, there were days when I felt like a squirrel in a cage, running round and round and getting nowhere in particular. But in those days life struck me most profoundly—the squirrel's cage was the best place to observe what others said and did, for then people hardly took notice of me when they talked about their lives. Envisioning myself in their place, I "graduated" from high school, as did my cousin, and "entered" the world and "met" new people; and together with the girl next door, I took a job, heard how it feels to get married, be pregnant, give birth, and have kids. I heard a lot about what makes people fail or succeed in life.

As I watched others going through various experiences, I learned that the world out there was throbbing with changes that no one seemed to escape. Such thoughts made me daydream of the future, which made me feel the most alive. Nothing human was foreign to me—as if a certain range of experiences were inherent to all, as if sooner or later everyone ended up in the same waters. And while some waded into treacherous depths, others merely skimmed the surface.

A significant change took place between me and my parents. They stopped treating me like a child. Instead of telling me what to do, they now discussed with me what needed to be done, and there was much to talk about at dinnertime. And as the days went round and round, home became an oasis removed from the turbulent events in the world outside. Slowly I realized that change was the keeper of patterns I was learning to read, and time merely marked the durations of the different phases in our lives.

One evening, I was already in bed, not sure whether awake or dreaming, when a gray barn owl glided onto my windowsill.

"Had a good day?" she asked softly.

"Yes…"

"Ready for tomorrow?"

"Yes…" Now fully aware of the owl's presence, I asked, "And how about you?"

"I slept most of the day, as usual."

"Is there much difference between sleeping during the day or at night?"

"Not really. Your clock never stops, and the world goes on, regardless of night and day." She fluffed her feathers.

Dozing off, I said, "Good to know…"

But the owl did not stop talking. "Even a mouse spends its life in a loop of time assigned to mice. And so do stones and cows and people and the stars and planets in their orbits—all their life spans are fixed in a time-loop allotted to their kind or species. Who knows? Maybe the universe itself is moving toward a marked ending to begin again. In circles, small and immense, every single thing in existence is constantly becoming something else—either more of itself, or part of some other thing. Nothing is ever gained in this world or lost or wasted."

"Not even my life?" I asked dreamily.

"Not even your life or my life, regardless of how insignificant they may seem. Continuity is at the heart of life, and change in time keeps the world in flux."

Saying this, the owl hopped onto my bed, stooped, and winked. I took the hint, climbed onto its back, and cuddled up in the soft neck feathers. She hopped onto the windowsill, spread her wings, and, leaning into the night, rose high above the sleeping world. Lulled by the rhythmic flap of wings, I fell asleep and woke up only when the first glimmer of light brushed my cheek.

The owl landed on the edge of a cloud under the tall rafters that held up the sky. Supported on sturdy light beams, the rafters cast an intricate network of shadows on the cloud. Human voices filled the air, the sing-song familiar—farther down, my ancestors were weaving the family tapestry, light beams spotlighting different work areas. They worked in groups: some were moving about, some were seated at the loom, and others were looking over their shoulders. Those sitting in a circle were spinning yarn and telling stories, repeating the old ancestral tales over and over again. Their fingers moved in rhythm, their elbows at acute angles.

I was to learn the intricacies of every task, starting with the spinning of yarn. Seeing Grandfather, I sat down on the empty chair beside him. Next to him sat his nephew who had died young. Seated on the other side of me was a woman in a lace bonnet, a face I'd seen in the family album, and next to her an old woman I didn't recognize. Dressed in attire of different eras, men, women, and children of various ages were spinning raw wool from a heap that lay inside the circle of chairs.

A middle-aged woman was telling a story, the pitch of her voice tinting the yarn crimson as it passed between her fingers. "Soon after Cousin Ursula left the house, the darkness of night fell upon her, and relying on the mare to find the way, she entered the forest she had to cross. Listening to the clip-clop of hooves, she did not dare rush the mare for fear of waking the bewitching powers that lived in the forest and led people astray. Our cousin had to bring back a black rose before the next evening."

"A very challenging task," another ancestor picked up the thread of the tale, an embroidered bonnet over her hair. As she spoke, the yarn between her nimble fingers spun blue-green. "Because the knight in whose garden the black rose grew was a disagreeable fellow, not easy to talk to, and that was the only place in the whole world where a black rose could be found—"

At this point a bearded man took over. "Ursula was about to leave the forest when a wildly screeching fury jumped in front of the mare, and as the horse backed up, Cousin fell to the ground. Cackling, the fury jumped onto her chest."

"You are not fit to see or touch the black rose," it shouted, poking its fingers into our cousin's eyes. And as the yarn in the teller's hands turned shocking pink, everyone's elbows started to move faster, balls of rainbow hues bobbed up and down in rhythm, and heads nodded in agreement.

"But then a good fairy leapt out of the forest to chase the bad one away," continued an ancestor wearing a leather cap, the yarn in his hands tinted red with excitement. "The two fairies were still wrestling when a rooster crowed, announcing sunrise, and so dear Ursula was saved."

"She knocked on the door of the knight's castle in time for breakfast, and no one knows how the conversation went at the table, but—" and as the yarn in the hands of the narrator turned yellow, the pretty ancestor sitting next to him continued.

"She had to leave without the curative rose because the rose was still speckled with moon spots, not yet pitch-black. Told to come back the next day, Ursula turned homeward—" As the teenage girl smiled to herself, the yarn in her hands turned a bright orange.

"And that evening a flag went up on the roof of our dear cousin's house, to announce that her ailing father was still alive," a teenage boy continued. "The household was still hopeful that the black rose would lift the spell that made him ill. The next morning Cousin

Ursula left early. Promising to ride as fast as she could, she mounted the mare and departed, humming a happy tune." The youngster saying these words was interrupted the moment the yarn passing through his fingers turned purple.

A young mother with a stillborn infant in her lap picked up the thread. "But she had a long way to go, and although the mare cantered, the journey took longer than expected. Before sunrise, Ursula was still in the forest where the bewitching good and bad fairies lived. Our brave cousin, the sixth granddaughter of Genghis Khan, rode faster." At this she started sobbing, and the yarn in the young mother's hands turned a somber violet.

The stout matron beside her broke the spell of sadness and continued the story. "Ursula passed through the forest unharmed and reached the castle safely. At the castle gate, the knight was waiting, and he took her to the rose garden where roses of many colors were blooming. But the black rose was nowhere to be seen."

As the yarn she spun turned moss green, another ancestor chimed in. "Cousin followed the handsome knight across the rose garden, and when they came to the darkest corner of a stone wall, he stopped. Still, the black rose was not there. Cousin Ursula looked at the knight. He assured her that the rose was in the black shadows, that she only had to reach for it."

"Bravely, she put her hand into the shadows, and when a thorn pricked her finger, she closed her hand and pulled. The rose in her hand was blacker than the black of night, the single leaf purple, the stem and the thorns blackened like silver, the thorn in her finger blood red." The yarn in the old man's hands spun a metallic sheen.

"Seeing that the rose had a taste for blood, our brave cousin clenched her fist tightly and let the thorn sink deep into her finger.

And without loosening her grip, she held the rose in her hand all the way back home."

At this point a sharp-nosed man wearing a philosopher's cap picked up the yarn. "All ended well," he said. "Cousin Ursula had obtained the curative flower by promising to marry the knight, and she brought the rose home in time. And as her father held it in his withered hand, the hand turned pink, the rose turned pale, and the lord of the house recovered."

But the telling of stories did not stop there, for another ancestor began, "Remember the spring when..." And so many other family stories were told many times over, and each time they went around in a slightly different way—the retelling of old tales unending, the continuity unbroken, the ever-changing pitch of voices spinning a great variety of colored yarn. When the story was sad—an ancestor dying in a foreign land of wounds, the plight of a child orphaned early in life—misfortune slowed the fingers, the balls of yarn swayed sadly from side to side, and the colors got darker and deeper until a cheerful episode brightened faces and colors again. And when the stories were gay—like the one about the third son of Amragan, the Turk, the progenitor of the family, who scared away the robbers by scratching the wall behind which he was hiding, or the quick-witted cousin who, with a small group of friends, tricked the invaders into entering the marshes where horses and men perished without a trace—words came fast, faces flushed, spools bobbed as if giggling, and colors acquired a cheerful shine.

While those seated in the circle were spinning and telling stories—polishing episodes of their collective memory like stones in a river—other ancestors walked around them with scissors in hand. As soon as a yarn acquired a certain shade, they snipped out a length of it without breaking the flow of words, and took it to those who worked at the loom.

My next task was to learn when a color was ripe for snipping and deliver it to the weaver who used that shade of yarn. A color matured when the pitch in the teller's voice reached its highest or lowest point, and when I learned to listen for it, I had no trouble matching that color to the one the weaver was using already.

Once I'd mastered this part of the task, I took a turn standing behind the weavers and watching what their fingers produced. Those of us standing over them followed the emerging designs, every shape and pattern evoking expressions of exuberant joy. Our vocal responses either aligned a series of individual patterns or grouped them into kaleidoscopic memory configurations of which the carpet's design consisted. Not a single strand of color was rejected, and not a single pattern was corrected, as all were incorporated and marveled at. Amazed at the power of words to give the most ordinary event a bedazzling shape, I jumped from weaver to weaver, exulting in this stage of the task.

Then it was my turn to contribute to the ancestral tapestry. Seated at a loom with an off-white string of yarn, I let my fingers do the work. The pattern my fingers created was an angular white patch leaning precariously forward, the broadside sharply jagged.

Waves of wind rattled the rafters and someone shouted, "It's hatched, the egg has hatched! The white bird is flying out to sea!"

The pattern I had just completed was of a white bird in flight. The myth came alive, and I jumped to my feet. But it was too late—the bird was nowhere to be seen.

Standing at the edge of the cloud, I looked down. Far below lay the gold of a hundred molten suns. And as I was looking at it, the glittering mass started to rise, and slowly it came up to my feet, washed around my ankles, and then receded just as gently. Not a ripple on the surface, not a ripple inside me. And the warm golden mass rose again—again up to my ankles, rising and falling over and over again at its own slow, pulsing pace.

A pebble under my toes pricked my attention. I picked up the pebble, wound the scent of my hair around it, and buried it under my feet, so future generations would know that others before them had witnessed the rise and fall of molten suns.

Stilled for a hundred years, I asked the Earth. "Are you there? Do you hear me?"

A breeze combed my hair.

8

In the Absence of Time

At home nothing had changed, and the changes in me were hardly noticeable to people around me. Once in a while, Mom would ask why I valued silence so much, but I assured her that I was all right. I did what was expected of me, I did not complain or ask for anything, and I appeared to be at peace with the world and myself. But that was not how I felt.

Strange things were happening to me at every turn. The other day in class, I was so taken by what the math teacher was explaining that, at a certain point, my mind took off; blazing white, it ran ahead of what he was saying, racing toward an answer, which, to my astonishment, was the correct one. A few days later, I was listening to my favorite tape when I started rapping—rhymed lines gushing to the beat of music as if floodgates inside me had opened. Surrendering to the moment at hand, like a fountain turned on full, I let the words come. There was no sense of duration, no waiting, no holding back, no volition. In this fissure of time, I was an instrument to energy that was rushing through me, instead of acting on me. Though fleeting, these leaps of my jetting mind left footprints: whatever I touched was changed, as if I were the agent of change—myself untouched, unchanged by what rushed through me. At once exhilarated and frightened, I didn't know what to do with this energy spilling forth so effortlessly, so abundantly.

A postcard we received from Uncle Jack bore a picture of a round ancient building surrounded by a wall. On the side of the abandoned structure was an entrance framed by shadows. Daydreaming, I opened the door, descended the steps, and entered a world forgotten.

The vaulted ceiling of this ancient chamber rested on sturdy shadows, the floor covered knee-deep with white flour. On my right was an immense brick oven, the light of blazing flames licking the chamber's ceiling. On my left stood an old plank table with utensils for baking bread, their sheen reflecting centuries of handling. There was a horn of plenty, big enough for me to crawl in, and next to it a chalice of embossed silver, and the measure for salt filled with dried tears of four generations. In a large cauldron the yeast was already bubbling, and on a bench beside the table stood a bottomless silver pail of spring water. Next to it was a rosewood scoop, its lip covered with hammered silver showing signs of repair. The tub for kneading dough was big enough to hold a season's harvest of grapes.

It was clear what I had to do. Picking up the rosewood scoop, I filled the horn of plenty with flour scooped off the floor. When it could hold no more, the horn swiveled and tipped toward the tub by itself. And so did the measure of salt, the cauldron of yeast, and the pail of spring water, all replenishing themselves instantly.

With the tub half full, I climbed in, and while holding on to the rim, I used my knees and heels to knead the dough and made enough dough for a hundred loaves. Then I swept the oven clean of embers, shoved in the loaves, rolled a huge flat stone over the opening, and, in darkness, sat down against the wall to rest.

"Is baking bread my destiny?" I wondered silently, disappointed.

"It only looks simple—looks simple," a voice from the depths of earth answered.

"Did I come this far to bake bread?" I asked.

"You were given gifts—gifts—you did not ask for, and baking bread is a way of giving back—back—to the world what you reaped in the wind on the run—the run," the voice echoed. "But it is you who has to till the soil, sow the seeds, and tend to their growing. It is you—you—you who has to reap the harvest, separate the grain from the chaff, and grind the grains into flour—grind the grains—the grains—And it is you who has to collect and dry the tears—dry the tears—tears of generations, grow the hopes to excite the dough, and dig the bottomless well. Once you have the ingredients on hand, you have—have to find the door behind which the transformation occurs—look and find—find—and build the fire and wait—wait—and wait for the embers to cool." Echoes sparkling in darkness, the voice continued, "What you see here is the most intimate gift of life—life's energy replenishing itself in everything you touch—touch."

"Is there a place for me in this?" I wondered out loud.

"You are an instrument to energy in passing. Nothing more—nothing—nothing more."

"I mean me, the person sitting here." I insisted.

"What you just said is but energy—energy animating certain parts of your brain."

"But the self…"

"Is energy in motion—in motion—plunging and swelling as it meanders and gathers and rises and leaps and falls, motion stirring sensations which make you feel alive—alive—alive. Whether a bird in flight, a rolling ocean wave, a thought, a book, hunger, or pain moves you, it's the sensation, which makes you aware of yourself and creates the illusion—illusion—that a self is there. There is no self, only the illusion of it."

"Then why this merry-go-round of experiences?"

"Experience carves the streambeds that collect your humanness. Experience informs—informs and directs the flow. You are unique only—only—in what you make of an impression, how you choose to respond to it—" The echoes were making me drowsy.

"But impressions are so…unpredictable…" I muttered, to keep the deep voice flowing.

"You have no objective, nothing to channel—channel your energy into. When it starts flowing into something you can lay your hands on, energy draining into the material shapes—shapes the material at hand."

"Am I responsible for what happens during this rush of energy or for the changes it brings?" I tried to rouse myself.

"The rush is innocent—innocent—of intent. It is blind—blind as the sap that splits the seed, unfolds the leaves, and pushes a bud to bloom—blind as the force that keeps the planets in orbit. You look—and look—and you look at the results and see what you have produced, and then choose—you choose what to keep and what to reject. In the choices you make lies the responsibility—" Now the echoes were hardly audible.

In a strange foreshortening of vision, the wide world funneled to a single point. There I stood, my mind in my hands. My mind was as malleable as clay: the responsibility for the direction my life was to take was mine alone—alone—alone.

The aroma of freshly baked bread woke me up, the inner clock ticking loudly. Suddenly hungry for home—for the simple pleasures

I'd learned to cherish—I unloaded the oven in a hurry, and racing up the flight of stairs, I brought the loaves outside to cool. Running back and forth, I stacked them in the yard in rows three loaves high, and was returning for more when the stillness around me whipped into rushes of wind. I turned in time to see the white bird descending like a shimmering cloud, the wings spanning a field. Landing outside the yard, it reached for the loaves, and from the shadows of the doorway, I watched it gorge itself on the bread. Having its fill, the bird took off.

Oh, how glad I was that I'd baked enough bread to last the bird for years!

It was time to go home, to return to where I belonged. Taking two loaves for the road, I started walking toward a grove of trees in the distance. In their shadow, sitting around a table, were men and women from many countries. Offered a seat on a bench, I placed the loaves on the table and sat down.

The people wanted to know where I'd been, and what I had seen. Each spoke in a different tongue, yet each was understood by all, the singsong of different languages bubbling likes a brook.

A young man asked me in Chinese, "Where did you come from?"

"From back there," I answered in Lithuanian, my mother's native tongue and was understood by everyone present.

"And where is bread to be found in these regions?" asked a woman in Serbian.

I turned to point and said, "I baked it myself in that domed building over there. Have some," I said, breaking a loaf and passing one half to the woman and the other to a young man beside her.

"Thank you," he said in Swahili. After breaking off a piece and passing the rest to the others, he asked, "And where are you going now?"

"Home. I want to go home," I said hastily.

In celebration, a white linen cloth was spread on the table, and as we broke the bread, wine was brought out and goblets were filled. Each time around the wine was older and stronger, from a jug more ornate, and the amount of the wine more generous.

"Does anyone know the way home?" I asked.

"I just came from there," said a young woman in Portuguese. A man added in Polish, "See the bushes behind the hillock? There you will find a flat stone and under the stone the exit."

Ready to leave, I stood up. "You should not go home empty-handed," said an old man in Nepalese. "Take the unbroken loaf with you."

I wished them all well, and, after exchanging farewells, I headed for the hillock. I found the stone under a bush, and when I moved it aside, a mirror-smooth pool the color of forget-me-nots stared up at me. Reflected in it were my face and the loaf of bread under my arm. Ready to break bread with one and all, I jumped in.

Epilogue

Some twenty years have passed. Let it suffice to say that after high school, I entered college and graduated after majoring in English. Then I got a job in a publishing house, and in my early twenties, I married David, a teacher. We had two children, a daughter Cara, who is now eleven, and a son Andrew, who is seven. We live in an old sprawling house, which we bought a few years ago. It is on the fringes of a large city, and in need of much repair. David works in the city. With both children in school, I work at home, editing books for a publishing company. I'm also writing a book of my own.

My dream adventures ended when I finished high school; college life was too consuming to think about the past. Since we settled into the new house, I've started thinking about those early wanderings and their effect on my life. Were they useful? Did I learn something, or were those dreams merely one other youthful flight, grounded for good by actual experience?

The other day I was looking for some papers and came across an old folder in which I found an outline of those dreamlike episodes, intended for some college assignment but never used. While leafing through the pages, I had the uncanny feeling that fragments of the dream experiences were popping up in my life to this day.

I had never spoken about my dream experiences to anyone and, curious as to whether the hunch was grounded, I decided to watch for them during the course of a day. Getting up one morning too early to wake the kids, I thought this was as good a day as any to track my activities and observe their effect on my inner states.

The morning started as usual. I poured myself a glass of juice, then lifted the kitchen window shades to check the weather. Noises from the upper floor signaled that Cara was in the shower, and I went upstairs to help Andrew find socks that would match his shirt, as he insisted. Back in the kitchen to start breakfast, I found David there, already dressed. We exchanged a few words, and as soon as the kids came down, the family fell into its usual breakfast routine. Each had an assigned task, and to avoid bumping into each other, we traced well rehearsed patterns on the kitchen floor: I was at the range making coffee and scrambling eggs; David was making toast and fetching things from the refrigerator; Cara was setting the dishes, flatware, and cereals on the table; and Andrew, after putting the napkins and glasses in their place, was sitting in his chair, waiting for us to join him. During breakfast, we shared what each of us expected to do that day. After breakfast was over, David left the table first to catch his bus for downtown. I helped the kids with their jackets and books, and off they went walking to school.

Though brief, this quiet ritual of synchronized movements put us all at ease. Time was not intrusive because we set our own pace: if we got up later, we moved faster; and if earlier than usual, we moved more slowly. The order of activities was firmly established and suspended our individualities. And though we were fully aware of each other's movements, each of us was also alone, wrapped in a world of their own. When we sat down to breakfast together, a sense of accomplishment made it easy to share what we expected to happen during the course of the day, and at that point we became individuals again.

Now alone in the house, I cleared the table, poured myself another cup of coffee, and sat down by the window in the kitchen alcove. This was the time when I reviewed what I planned to accomplish during the day, and I cherished those minutes. This morning, however, I didn't linger long; the prospect of working on my book made me eager to start the day.

I made the beds, took a shower, and dressed. I then sat down at my desk, hoping to spend the morning hours working on the book I was writing. After rereading what I had written yesterday, I was ready to continue.

Hardly an hour into writing, I glanced over what I had just written. I changed one word, then another, which prompted me to rewrite the last three paragraphs, which shifted the direction the plot was to take. Suddenly charged by clarity of mind and trusting the moment at hand, I started writing furiously. Words were gushing forth at such a speed that the plot shift was now running like a red thread through page after page. I slowed down and stopped only when a slack wave of exhaustion washed over my mind. The rush had lasted for an hour, yet it seemed that only minutes had passed. When I looked at the results, I found many surprises—gifts I neither asked for nor dreamt of.

Somewhat disoriented by the experience, to steady my mind I made a list of groceries to be bought before the kids came home. Then I called the plumber to check on whether he was coming this afternoon as scheduled. Ready to move on, I picked up the book I was editing and had barely started when a friend called to tell me about the spat she had had with her husband that morning. Though aggravated by the interruption, I listened politely. What upset me most about her calls was the commiseration I was drawn into merely out of friendship. Flashes of the meadow pit made me cut the call short.

After lunch, I returned to editing the book. With pencil in hand, I curled up in my favorite chair and, expecting to work for the next two hours, plunged into the verbal constructs of another mind. This kind of work challenged my ability to detect the hidden causes and effects by which the author had constructed the plot, something I was interested in as a writer myself.

I was deeply immersed in the work when the plumber arrived. When he came up from the basement, he said he was not going to touch the pipes under the kitchen sink, for fear that the main pipe rising from the basement might collapse. Refusing to do a patch-up job, he promised to have an estimate in a couple of days.

The news hit me hard, for we had just completed repairs on the roof, and the loan we'd taken to pay for it was already stretching our budget. Making ends meet was our most pressing concern, and an added expense could complicate matters considerably.

After the plumber left I called another company for a second opinion, then left a message for David. He called me back, and, after hearing what the plumber had said, he suggested I contact a third company for a complete picture of the situation. He then asked me whether I could manage to live with it for a while—put a larger bucket under the sink or something. This upset me even more, for an unfixed leak can get only worse, increasing the expense.

As I hung up, I was disgusted with the whole situation to such an extent that I was ready to drop everything and stop trying to cope with such petty demands that sapped so much of my energy. Well-aware that this would not solve the problem, I asked myself, should

I stop writing my book and look for a job? Maybe the publishing house could give me more freelance work?

To find out what my chances were, I called a friend at the publisher's office and learned that things were slow this season. That tightened the screw, and a glance at the clock reminded me that I had to go shopping before the children got home. While driving I thought of the direction my life had taken.

Family was the anchor that gave me comfort, purpose, and steadied my mind. But my so-called writing career, was another matter. Though it was daunting, writing gave me a respite from the world and forced me to think through many puzzling issues. In other words, writing helped me to live. Why, then, was I unsure of whether I was on the right track? I remembered Gloria, another freelancer I'd met at the office, who was also working on a book, and decided to call her later that afternoon.

I finished with shopping sooner than I had expected, and on my way home I stopped at the bank and found there a line long enough to discourage anyone. Deciding to stay and see how fast the line moved, I was soon thinking, "Who has the time for this?"

A woman turned and said, "I have a small child in the car..." "The inefficiency of clerks these days..." added another. "Its insulting," the man behind me finished the sentence. Most of us were irritated—many fidgeting—some leaving the line already. Soon, I too was thinking that I had more important things to do, but realizing that I had ten extra minutes to spare, I decided to take it in stride. I did make it to the teller, and, in a cheerful frame of mind, I made it home just before the children walked in.

I called Gloria. A lot was on the burner in her life, and everyone in her circle was actively engaged in something or other. Excited to hear from me, she asked if I could come on Thursday evening to a reading her writing group was giving at her place, and she invited me to join the group. I promised to think it over and call her back, but then and there decided that a change in routine would do me good.

And suddenly, in spite of the plumbing, I was in a festive mood, ready to cook a special dinner, and cheer up my husband as well. Eager to indulge in the delights cooking offered, I called Cara, and while we peeled and washed the potatoes, carrots, onions, parsnips, and celery stalks, we talked about what it means to live fully and about the so-called art of living: a headline she'd seen in a magazine at the dentist's office. Was there such a thing or was it mere talk? "If people are talking about it, there must be something to it," Cara said.

"Let's see," I mused. "Any kind of achievement requires practice and skill. Art also calls for total immersion in the moment at hand, for letting go of everything else in your mind and concentrating on the work alone. To reach that level of concentration takes effort, and to keep one's attention focused on one thing for a prolonged period of time calls for discipline."

"Discipline?" asked Cara.

"Yes, discipline. Discipline acts like the banks of a river that keep water running in a certain direction, instead of it spilling all over the place. Discipline concentrates attention on what is going on this very minute, and it prevents you from wasting your time and energy."

"Aren't we doing this now?"

"Yes, we are," I smiled.

"That's not so difficult," observed Cara.

By then the vegetables were cut into cubes and disks and wedges, ready for the pot. Cooked and pureed, they would make David's favorite soup that was served with garlic bread, which Cara buttered herself. The sauce we were making of dried mushrooms we picked in Canada last summer was to go with the broiled beef and mashed potatoes. Enticing aromas brought Andrew downstairs, and my attention was so focused on tasting and seasoning the sauce that I was startled when David walked into the kitchen.

"Smells good! What are we celebrating tonight?" he asked.

"Oh, nothing in particular. We felt like having something special to cheer us up."

At the table the mood was festive, and we chatted about the events of the day at school and at work. The plumber was not mentioned until the children were upstairs doing their homework.

"I don't think we should take out another loan," said David.

"Agreed. We shouldn't," I answered. "Why don't we wait for the estimates and then see what must be done? I'd rather not talk about it tonight."

"Agreed," said David, and he turned to leave the kitchen.

But before leaving, he came over to me at the sink, and standing behind me, he put his arms around my waist and kissed my cheek. "Thank you for the supper," he whispered.

My hands in soapy water, I leaned against his chest. Holding me tight, David said, "See you later."

We watched the news on TV in silence. Assignments completed, the kids joined us, and we cuddled up on the sofa for the evening. There was nothing good on TV, so David put on a CD of medieval chants. A clear, pure voice filled the room with majestic, distant spaces and transported each of us into our own intimate musings. I was besieged by images of that huge, glowing sphere of water bobbing on top of the water wall.

Andrew was soon asleep, and Cara followed us upstairs to watch me put her brother to bed. While Cara slipped into her pajamas, I turned down her bed, picked up the clothing from her chair, kissed both children goodnight, and joined David in the living room. He was already immersed in the plot of a movie, and so the day came to an end.

Lying awake in bed that night, I wondered what made me shift gears—change frames of mind that often?

Every shift was triggered by a change in the surroundings. The shift had nothing to do with my past or the people around me, but it was related directly to my surroundings—how I saw myself then and there, and what the situation did to me. That notion of self, however, did not carry over when the situation changed; for regardless of whether I felt in control of it or was thrown off balance by it, every time the surroundings changed, I had to adjust to what was there. I had to accept the setting and behave accordingly or feel awkwardly out of place. That shift in outlook gave me a grip on the situation—it placed the situation in a perspective that, in turn, adjusted my frame of mind and changed my behavior. One thing was certain, whether I related to things near or far set the pace of my activities: the near clamored for immediate attention, the far relaxed the urgency. Since no one else could possibly know how at any given moment I related to a situation, when sensing time I faced the world alone. Thus as soon as I'd notice that something had changed outside of or inside me, I was compelled to switch time concepts like gears. But when I failed to notice a change and held on to a prevailing mind-set, habit took over. And then I would tackle events with unfit rigging, unsuitable sensors, and unmatched faculties, frustrating the effort. As a means to personal orientation, nothing surpassed the seven perceptions of time.

Events of the day started rolling through my mind. Getting ready for school and work slipped by hardly noticed. I had no doubt that during our breakfast we were firmly in circular time, enjoying the activities that enabled us to have breakfast together. It never failed to amaze me how the synchronization of movements not only eased the task but also united us in spirit; how, when working as a group, we suspended our personal concerns, if only for a while. Alone in the house after breakfast, I was ready to plunge into personal time and reconnect with that nebulous core of my being known to me alone.

At my desk, I recalled making revisions and pushing words through the belabored tunnels of thought—a slowly twisting discomfort suddenly leaping into a clarity of mind. As if something inside me—something that existed in me long before but lay dormant—had reawakened and propelled my mind and my hand into action at a speed that blocked out all thought. There was no volition, no sense of duration, or of time passing; speed was the indication that I was merely an instrument, a conduit to energy passing through me. Action took place in the absence of time, and the results were a total surprise to the observing mind. Maybe this activity shouldn't be called work, for it was some kind of a coming together of parts already there but unconnected before.

When the gush was over, to steady my mind, I'd made a list of groceries. Now poised in clock time, my mind was rummaging through memory, selecting the items and ingredients I had to pick up at the supermarket.

That mind-set had been broken by the neighbor eager to talk about the spat with her husband. She'd found a friendly ear, and on this morning commiseration—a weakness of mine—had disturbed me immensely. Visions of the pit in the meadow, with Auntie's face leaning into mine, made my stomach churn. I got up, had a glass of water, and, feeling better, went back to bed.

As I snuggled under the covers, I returned to reliving the events of my day. After lunch I'd worked on the book assigned by the office. Now squarely in clock time, I'd analyzed the manuscript, paragraph by paragraph, with reason as an irreplaceable tool. And then the plumber arrived, and as I was listening to him in a rational frame of mind, the bad news pulled the floor out from under my feet. Stopped cold, I tried to adjust. Besieged on all fronts by threatening demands, I suddenly realized why in the River of Time you are in a war zone. When survival is at stake, you forget the future, for there is no time for dreams and there is no time for scruples when your existence is threatened—one grabs what is at hand hoping to relieve the immediate pressure.

I must admit that at this point listless time, and the comfortable withdrawal from the world it offered, loomed over me like an attractive solution. While savoring the allure of isolation, I shuddered at how ready I was to drop the world and spin a cocoon around me.

I'd been saved from these gloomy thoughts by the idea that getting a job would help, and the switch from time stilled back to clock time had brought relief. But while driving to the supermarket, thoughts of my future made me slip into personal time. In that frame of mind, I was in an ancient sanctuary, the quick of my being under the *oculus,* listening for those elusive echoes that enlarge or diminish my stature and make more or less of me. This contact with the most intimate and responsive core of my being has never failed to restore a sense of security, quite apart from the security a full-time job would offer. Shopping went fast. Feeling welcome in the market and familiar with the layout of the store, I'd pace myself and run through the list as fast or as slowly as I wanted. But when, with my mind set in clock time, I'd stepped into the bank and saw the line, it felt as if the world itself had conspired against me. The bank was not accommodating its clients, and the setup was forcing me to accept the inadequate service that clashed with the rhythm of my inner state—the aggravation pressing me to decide whether to resign to the situation or leave the bank. Any other action would be ineffective, and that made me feel helpless and insignificant.

My refusal to change gears made standing in line frustrating. But when I realized that I had some time to spare, and, instead of watching the clock, instead of resisting to accept the set up, I chose to flow with the situation, suddenly both the frustration and the aggravation lifted. It hadn't been a matter of patience, resignation, or submissiveness. By changing my outlook, I switched time concepts, and, by using those ten minutes to review my personal concerns, I spent the waiting time meaningfully. I took control of the situation by putting myself outside of the bank's regulations.

The experience boiled down to a simple fact—when I'm on the run or my mind is racing, the world appears to be standing still, and, when the mind disconnects from the surroundings, the world rushes by unnoticed. But when you change your focus, the world "adjusts." What a difference a slight mental shift can make!

Talking to Gloria had raised glimmers of hope, mainly of change, which uplifted my spirit. And then Cara and I cooked and talked and had a jolly time in the kitchen. The handling of colorful roots, the shapes cool and plump in my hand; the sharp knife cutting them into neat slices and cubes; the crunchy textures; the earthy smells and tastes; and the singsong of our voices—all the little things that held us captive in the here and now were richly rewarding. As lines of separation between mother and daughter faded, a tide of friendship washed over Cara and me, and the afternoon passed swiftly. The festive mood was not accidental.

Then Andrew and David joined us in the kitchen, and, when we sat down to supper, the flow of affection was not disrupted. Throughout the afternoon and at dinner, each of us was responding and responsive to the other; the family was firmly grounded in the absolute here and now.

I clearly remember how after supper I'd avoided changing gears—talk of plumbing would switch my mind to clock time and cut short the mood of the evening. Though there was no avoiding the subject, David and I were glad to drop it. Why disturb the flow of a good feeling? Why not let it run its course? Didn't this all-embracing gut feeling underlie most human yearnings?

How do you describe what goes on in the head when time changes faces?

The five senses are windows through which the towering head receives impressions and so instructs the mind of what goes on in the surroundings. In the here and now, the senses pull the strings, and the world comes in like a blast of wind. Besieged by impressions, my mind identifies with whatever takes it for a ride; runaway thoughts have a similar effect. In the River of Time, the going gets tough, and the drive to survive kicks in. Helpless to change the surroundings or the situation, I focus attention on whatever threatens my survival, and then defensive and aggressive actions are the norm.

There is, however, also the tendency to retreat into the safety of pits and complain about the human condition. In clock time the outlook is tainted by belief, conviction, or experience, which, like stained glass windows of colorful interpretations, filter or obscure sensory impressions and so cushion the impact of the surroundings. On the road carefully-mapped, the rational mind pulls the strings. In listless time the windows are bolted from the inside to shut out all sensory activities. Disengaged, I become unresponsive to the world and to others as well. In personal time the barriers between the inner and outer worlds are removed. Ready to take off in any direction, I am on the lookout for cues that might advance a personal cause, aim, or dream. Since the road is unmapped and the chances are erratic, I have to make decisions on the spot. In circular time the inner and outer worlds interlock. Their dynamic interaction and the interdependence between the two realities nurture them both. And in the absence of time, internal forces pull the strings, and, overwhelmed by forces that well up to burst within, the mind is stripped of will—merely a conduit for the energy flowing toward whatever is at hand. The mind regains willpower when the gush is over. In all situations, choice, that tricky flip of mind, makes my behavior and my actions either constructive or destructive.

Though drowsy, I still could see how sips of morning coffee make me savor the flavors of the here and now. Or I slip into personal time for a navigational overlook—as to where I am in relation to some projected dream or goal—to learn whether I'm getting closer to or drifting away from it. When problems arise I am squarely in the River of Time as I tackle them, and in the pits when debating which approach to take, but I switch to clock time when planning ahead. When I'm overwhelmed or sapped by a situation, I stagnate in listless time, withdrawing from the world either to recollect myself or to gain a detached overview. I tend to experience the absence of time in the heat of work, and I relax in circular time on the cushions of civilization—listening to music, reading a book, or watching a movie or a ballgame.

What had I learned? I had learned that time is not fixed but elastic—its plasticity due to the mind's ability to focus on and adjust to internal and external changes, to see the same situation from a different angle. And though a shift of view eliminates all other views, in the act of adjusting, I merely shift the focus of my attention to give me a better grip on what has changed and then tailor an approach most suitable to the situation. Only now did I realize that this shifting from one viewpoint to another is an ongoing exercise in personal survival, physical as well as mental. Every successful resolution is a fresh beginning—life's continuity merely changes direction or form.

And then I had one other foreshortening of vision: the rift between the two realities—the intangible world of sensations, feelings, and dreams, and the tangible reality of the waking hours—was fused like the two sides of a coin, some alchemy welding them into an interdependent, indivisible whole. Is that all there is to it?

And what would this question answer? It would merely remove the question mark and affix a temporary label to what the question was about. Aren't most answers merely one of many possible answers, with none writ in stone and all changing in time and culture?

In the stillness of the night, I wondered how would Cara and Andrew fare in a world that marches to the same clock—to the exclusion of others—in a world where inner clocks were ignored and even shunned. Would they be mesmerized by cyberspace and virtual reality? Would they glorify technology, artificial intelligence, and genetic engineering? Would they be besieged by ever more perplexing questions? And who will answer them, when investigations supersede each other nonstop and overwhelm us with information that merely boggles imagination? In this age of information, every twitch of a thought is filtered through someone else's opinion—aren't we forgetting how to think for ourselves? How to simply be human?

That night I dreamt that I was back in the house of Mary, my high school friend. Though I was in my teens, my children stood beside me. Together we were looking at the small white skulls aligned across the front of the black T-shirt Linda had spread on Mary's bed. Andrew was counting them aloud, "One, two, three, four," and then he stopped. Every time he said a number out loud, the word erased the skull he'd counted.

"Why did you stop?" asked Cara, "Go on," she insisted, pointing to the remaining skulls.

"I can't," said Andrew, staring at them. "There is no life where there is no death."

Startled, I woke up. How come Andrew's answer sounded like a profound confirmation of life? It was change—change the redeeming force, change which secured continuity, change the constant that made things new and kindled hope!

With a sigh of relief, I turned in bed. Good night—sleep well—dream—

THE END

0-595-33536-5